PHILANTHROPY

An Inspired Process

Mike Skrypnek

Bound Publishing

BOUND
PUBLISHING

Bound Publishing

United States
6501 E. Greenway Pkwy
#103-480
Scottsdale, AZ
85254

Canada
Suite 114
720 28th St. NE
Calgary, AB T2A 6R3

Toll Free Phone and Fax: 1-888-237-1627
Email: info@boundpublishing.com
Web: www.boundpublishing.com

ISBN (hardcover): 978-0-9867233-4-6
ISBN (ebook): 978-0-9867233-5-3

Library of Congress Control Number: 2010917187

Cover: Mark Dittmer
Text: Anamarie Seidel; Finely Finished, LLC
Edit: Michelle Baer & Bound Publishing

DEDICATION

To my parents,
my wife Sherri,
and our children
Madison and Coen.

Your unconditional love
and unwavering support
have been my inspiration.

CONTENTS

PREFACE

You've done well, right? Better than well? You've built a business or two, accumulated a little wealth. People look up to you. They respect your accomplishments. It is possible that the lives of tens or even hundreds of people have benefited from your vision, business acumen, dedication and perseverance. You have been a company builder, an entrepreneur, a pretty great person overall. You could say you've made a difference, had an impact. Your hard work and efforts have made some lives better.

Well, have you really? What have you actually done to leave your mark in this world? Will the janitor working the night shift at the plant you own remember you once you've left? You might never have actually met the man. How about the others who helped you build your own success? What did you ever do for the woman beaten by her husband at home while supporting two kids, showing up for your forty-hours-a-week data entry cubicle job with two weeks' vacation? She worked diligently, mostly because she had to in order to pay her mounting bills, and she was there faithfully every day—sometimes because it was safer to be working than to be home with her husband. Did you know she needed your help? More help than you could personally handle? Of course you might have helped if you knew, right? How could you have known? When you think about it, did you change your community? Did you change the world? Can you?

How have you given back? Or have you even started?

When we look in the mirror, most of us know we could do better. We could do more to help others. In fact, a lot of the time we feel a little bad that we haven't done more. But where do we start? What is the point? The problems you think really need fixing don't seem to go away, anyways.

There's always more suffering, there's never a cure and there's no shortage of dysfunction and pain out there. You've already made a name for yourself in your life and your business; you're certainly not looking for fame. But then again, fading into anonymity doesn't make much sense either, especially if you hope to be a role model or leader. It's almost a requirement to be known for your giving in order to mentor or set an example for others. You can throw your money at a cause, have a wing of a hospital dedicated in your name or in the name of a loved one, and hope the organization you select for your charitable donations has the right people for the job. Spread your money around generously and often to a number of areas or charities and you're really giving, right?

Some of you might consider yourselves to be quite philanthropic, and you might very well be correct. I'm certainly not here to judge you. If you give, in any way, it is a good thing. But let me suggest that the size of the cheque you write or gift you give does not define your philanthropy. It is through your involvement in the gift or critical selection of those who will steward the funds and deploy them skillfully and passionately to further the cause that your philanthropy is defined. Research and oversight are required, and they take time and knowledge that you might not possess right now. And of course, if you never let anyone know you are doing this, what influence will you have on others who are looking for a leader and a role model? How can you inspire others to follow your example?

I'll tell you straight out that my goal in writing this book is to inspire you, to motivate you and to enlighten you. I want to push or pull you along. I am hoping to provide a little guidance, some insight and maybe that inspiration for you to look deeper into your giving. Through my research for this book, I have become more inspired, too. I know I can do better, and I know I will work harder to do so.

I have learned that giving is easy for most people, and it is done all over the world every day. Drop a few cents in the Salvation Army pot, buy a book of coupons from the student who comes to your door, even adopt a family at Christmastime or enter a charity running event in your community. Lend a hand to a neighbor or coach your kids' soccer team. All very obvious and commonplace ways millions of people give, every year. But in your life, it's been said that you're not common, and you've certainly never been one to consider yourself just another anonymous member of a large crowd. You have worked years to differentiate yourself and your business. Your giving has been purposeful and significant, but then again, it has not been so intrusive as to disrupt your day-to-day life. It has fit very well within the context of your life at the right times for you. Let me tell you, though, giving in most forms is easy. Intentional philanthropy is an entirely different ball game.

Philanthropy—what does it mean? Why is it different than giving? Well, I don't think providing you with a definition of the word at this point and time is necessary. I will get to that later, for sure. I have found that philanthropy that really makes a difference is a process. It is the sequential execution of important steps in an effort to make the world a better place. It does sound a little bit more cold and methodical than one would expect, but that is where first impressions can be deceiving. The process of philanthropy is personal. It is empowering. It is a little scary at times, and it most definitely is rewarding. We will discuss the meaning of the word later on, but first we need you to think of your past history of giving, as it might serve as a good starting point. There is much work to be done—much great work to be done. Let's get to it.

You have seen and may even have been a part of greatness. The things you've accomplished might have only been accomplished by very few people. So how can you use these accomplishments to really make a difference? How do you translate your skills, knowledge, connections and money into a legacy that changes the world?

Don't worry; I'm going to help show you how. I'll give you the simple tools and the fundamental understanding that you and your team can utilize to form your own strategic philanthropic initiative. I'll highlight essential motivations and the top reasons for giving. You'll find they are a constant inspiration to many who devote themselves to philanthropy.

You'll see some different ways in which you can give; I'll explain what the most sensible strategy is for someone in your circumstances. I'll give you some step-by-step plans. You will quickly understand what you need to be looking for in the organizations you want to support. They must have specific qualities and characteristics that enhance their ability to get the job done. I will start by giving you well-known examples of those people who have made the conscious decision to pursue philanthropy that is staring you right in the face today. I will show you how great leaders and people with great purpose, like you, committed to certain decisions and acted upon them with single-minded focus, becoming extraordinary people and, in some cases, global icons.

You will be compelled to join them.

ACKNOWLEDGMENTS

My gratitude for all I have been given and all the opportunity I have before me should be first extended to my parents. Mom and Dad, you have given me the confidence and the human tools to achieve success. Your perseverance through life and never ending optimism has provided a road map for my life.

Sherri, I want to thank you with all my heart for your love and rock solid loyalty. You "get" me like no one has. You have been my biggest fan and supporter. You are always there to guide me through self-doubt. Sherri, you always said I should write a book. This topic stirred a passion in me to go through with it.

To Madison and Coen, I might be your Superman, but, until you have children of your own, you won't understand how much you have changed my life. My passion and direction have stemmed from your very existence.

I also would like to thank the many, many people, who were so gracious to allow me to grill them, and interview them privately about their philanthropy and their thoughts on the challenges and successes they have lived while giving of themselves. It was through these discussions that my journey took a different turn and things ended in a much better place than where they started. You know who you are and I cannot express my appreciation enough.

Finally I would like to thank some other people who were critical in writing this book, including Michelle Baer. Michelle your guidance and schedule kept me on track, but I am still not entirely sure whether you *really* think I can write, or if you just wanted to help me find my way as an author. I want to thank my Richardson GMP contingent for their support. Grant and Andrew I appreciate the bigger picture you see and the patience you have extended to me to develop my business. Tammy and Susan, you have been incredible.

For teaching me some very personal lessons, along this journey, I want to thank Michael, Birgitte and Colin and Ryan. You have given me courage to share and embrace the strength in vulnerability.

Can You Spot the
PHILANTHROPIST?

A Local Story of a Leader Who is Rising to Extraordinary Heights

People in Calgary and across Canada gained respect for Brett Wilson for his commitment as a business leader and as a key player in North American energy markets. Brett became a great leader of a great niche firm in the oil and gas industry in Canada, FirstEnergy Capital Corp., a powerhouse firm that, back in 1993, people suggested was too specialized to survive, let alone become an industry leader.

Over the years, giving became an ongoing pursuit for Wilson, alongside his business. His annual client appreciation events raised large sums for his corporate foundation, which in turn were donated to various community organizations. At one point along the way, though, his personal journey overshadowed his business, having a crucial impact on his path to philanthropy: his successful battle with prostate cancer became a critical juncture. While giving had always been a part of Wilson's life and had been instilled into his company, it was at this crossroads that Brett made the decision to direct the projects he was involved in to some higher purpose. He was blessed with excellent financial circumstances, but he knew that in order to make a difference, he could not merely throw money at the issues. He had to focus his attention on his causes with the same critical thinking and determined energy that had made his business a success. Unabashed philanthropy became a way of life, and business was a part of that effort.

Today Brett devotes a large part of his time and money to promoting charitable causes, raising funds and critical awareness for prostate cancer. Simultaneously he has begun to develop somewhat of a celebrity persona, which may provide him with greater influence and reach to further his philanthropic message and cause. He has given back to the community of Calgary in many ways over the years and has more recently focused his efforts on developing business programs and supporting the arts in Saskatoon, Saskatchewan. Brett made his most high-profile splash in the non-profit sector a few years ago when he spearheaded a fiftieth birthday celebration for himself and a number of his close friends. This group of fifty-year-olds happened to consist of some of Calgary's (and Canada's) wealthiest entrepreneurs and oilmen. The event raised over $3 million for prostate cancer in only one evening[1]. Brett's ability to influence and inspire those in the business community in Calgary reached a pinnacle at that moment. It was inspiring how effective the philanthropic initiative was at bringing together those powerful men in a common effort, also compelling many people from different viewpoints to join in the event. The unifying effect of the cause and the bold direction taken by Brett were likely much different than anything from his past capital markets experience.

The notoriety Brett has garnered has allowed him to use his expertise and position to influence others. That was just the beginning for him, and he soon looked toward spreading his message nationally. The question is, can and will he continue to utilize his newfound personality to further his philanthropy?

I have admired Brett's efforts for some time. I sit here today writing that I have observed his actions and have truly become inspired. He retains the caring, charitable core of his being even while starring on a television program pitting small business owners and entrepreneurs against shrewd venture capitalists looking to invest in new, up-and-coming businesses. The show, called the Dragon's Den (the CBC-run, Canadian version of the Shark Tank program on ABC), has a panel of venture capitalist cutthroat multi-millionaires like Kevin O'Leary, Arlene Dickinson, Robert Herjavec and Jim Treliving[2]. Wherever Brett has an opening, he delivers a meaningful and positive message. One episode showcased a far-out entrepreneur named Clayton with a very unique presentation for holistic vibrational healing and a message of sharing love with the world. The majority of panelist capitalists balked, ridiculing the presenter and his ideas openly and almost cruelly. Brett saw more. Having had to expand his conventional thinking on spirituality and healing in his own fight against cancer, Brett had experienced some of the holistic vibrations this entrepreneur was speaking of. He shared a small investment of $5,000 and, even more importantly, some personal time creating vibrations with the Tibetan bowls Clayton had demonstrated on the show. Brett provided him with some mentoring guidance, but mostly he took part and showed an interest in the man's life and learned a bit from him as well. Brett embraced the softer, inclusive side of the entrepreneur's character in a way that his peers really could not understand. Brett knew, though, that everyone draws their own path and derives their own comforts and strengths from different and, for some, very unconventional places.

In some of my reading, one thing that struck me was that Brett has mentioned he was influenced by Sir Richard Branson and considers him a mentor, a great modern philanthropist and iconic personality in his own right. Most would say that Sir Richard Branson is one of the world's most interesting capitalists and serial entrepreneurs with a major social conscience.

As for Brett and his commitment to doing good, living in pursuit of a truly philanthropic life, he is on the cusp of taking an enormous leap beyond his own imagination and will someday be able to look back and know he changed the world in a meaningful way. The abundance that will flow back to him will be substantial. Lives will be better because Brett made a decision to make them so.

A Tale of Two Roads Travelled

For some, philanthropy becomes a conscious choice when they are faced with their own mortality due to a sudden illness. For some, philanthropy is the culmination of personal experiences and triumphs, and for others it is the stark realization that our time on earth is lived in a blink of an eye and that very few people leave a lasting legacy. Others may have never considered the possibility of leaving a lasting legacy, or maybe they have, but consciously decided not to pursue it.

Let's talk about an example of a person who might never have picked up this book. They are different than you in this. They did not realize that philanthropy was a natural next step for them. This man worked tirelessly through a long career, lived a fairly charmed life and, at seventy years of age, never suffered what anyone would consider real loss. The man's parents were alive and well, in their nineties. His children were well, his wife was healthy and happy, they had no pets and most good friends were alive and active.

After forty years of working in his profession, he was sitting on tens of millions of dollars—more money than he could use or his children needed. When pressed for what he would do with all that money, he said that at his age, he wasn't sure he'd do anything major, as he was concerned he might actually run out of money before he died. He had his wife and himself to worry about. His family, including his adult children and grandchildren, were all very well taken care of. They didn't need his money, and besides, how would a handout help them, or anyone for that matter?

Well, what about charity? He gave. How? He gave to a charity and he had served on the board or committees of that same charity for more than a decade. He seemed to have a genuine concern for the cause, but after a closer look, it was apparent his motives might be different from those of others who were dedicated to the cause. The mandate of the organization was to save ecologically sensitive land, thus preserving habitat for wildlife, throughout North America. But loving and protecting the land had an advantage. The preservation efforts of the organization worked very well and resulted in fertile hunting grounds; animals and birds thrived in their habitats. The ironic thing was that the man was a passionate hunter.

Now don't misinterpret my obvious bias. I am not a fan of hunting at all, but I'm not condemning him for being a sportsman and having a passion for it, or anyone for actually choosing hunting as a hobby. Whether I agree with it or not, I understand that many people love hunting and fishing. What I will suggest is that I question his motives for choosing this organization and giving his time and money to it. I found that his motives were quite conflicted, and his preservation efforts were self-serving. They may have served as a way to directly conserve the land he was hunting or fishing on, or they may have been inspired by a desire to offset his obvious impact on the animal population or maybe even assuage a little of his guilt. As for money, he would match every thousand dollars donated by his friends to the charity, and he raised thousands of dollars while doing so.

Were there any other plans in his life, or beyond, to give? No, not really. When reviewing the succession of his estate, there was no desire to discuss planned giving or bequeathing so that some of his wealth could be directed to his most meaningful cause. He had not made any decisions to leave any of his money to charity at all. The fact was that he truly believed he would not have enough money to last the rest of his life for himself and his wife, and he was unable to decide whether giving was important to him or whether he wanted to do more for the community. He didn't want to give much at that point because he needed to be sure he had enough to live on.

Then a sudden, unexpected illness took him and he died. His family grieved their loss, buried him and divided up the estate. No one else remembered much about him or even knew him for much beyond his business and his hunting and fishing accomplishments. Those who worked with the man never felt he was really looking out for their interests. They didn't really trust him much; his actions seemed driven by self-interest. He had no real higher purpose in life. He delivered no great impact outside of his own small world. He created no legacy and died rich, with the means to make a world of difference.

There are many cases in history of people who might have fit this profile. Quite frankly, this is not all that bad. Everyone has their reasons for giving and everyone is free to act how they feel is best for them. That said, not everyone has the financial means and the time or connections to make a major difference.

I'm not entirely sure what keeps someone from taking the next step to develop their philanthropic interests. Sometimes it is their upbringing, fear, or the complete lack of awareness of the possible impact that a conscious act of giving could have prevent those who are able to give from doing so. That lack of awareness, in itself, is unfortunate, and the opportunity to lead and become a visible role model to inspire others to contribute is lost forever. In fact, there are many who would consider the ramifications of being involved in philanthropy to be an intrusion in their life. For others, placing their interests in charity might identify them with a cause, thus revealing their own vulnerabilities to the community or the world. Or it might link them to causes they are passionate about that might not be shared or popular with many people. Their lack of willingness to face or expose a weakness or sympathy for others who might have suffered challenges similar to theirs may prevent noticeable or meaningful involvement. This private suffering can be paralyzing. What is worse, it can perpetuate through generations.

In many cases, a community leader who might have suffered from something controversial like child abuse, sexual abuse or a stigmatized mental illness would rather keep their experiences a family secret than openly support an organization that addresses such things, as it could link them directly to the truth about themselves and draw public attention to their disadvantaged or painful past. For some, the fear of loss of status or peer recognition is too much to bear, and thus they remain anonymous donors or even non-donors. This is really a lost chance to lead, but in some cases it can be quite understandable.

Now let's get back to the good stuff—creating a lasting legacy. Name the greatest philanthropists in North American history and you'll have a long list of recognizable people who have been gone a long time— Carnegie, Rockefeller, Ford, the Rothschilds, Vanderbilt and Astor, to name a few. Their legacies are deeply rooted in American history and are well known. None of them stumbled upon philanthropy. They made clear and long-term plans, led by their visions of helping people or making the world a better place.

Let's look at those leaders of society who made the conscious decision to give, to make a difference, to truly become philanthropists. What made them great was that they acted with intention. We will find that their legacy lasted beyond their lives and through many generations. In fact, their influence has played a major role in some of today's greatest charitable endeavors and in the continuance of major philanthropic efforts. Their funding and influence as well as their original intent has lasted generations. Their legacy has been purveyed through family, through business partners and their families, and through those whose lives were positively and permanently affected by their good deeds. We will also find that their wealth and influence continued to grow exponentially after they fully committed to their philanthropy and even beyond their lifespan.

CONTEMPORARY ICONS
Leaders Who Became Philanthropists

I am certain you all know about those who have passed on great legacies. They were great in their lives and their reputations grew after they died. Lasting legacy is something that drives many philanthropists and appears to have been a common goal for many wealthy people decades ago. Whether because of the disproportionately large amount of wealth created for so many in the western world or because of a greater global consciousness, purpose has shifted in modern times to emphasize living legacies. The premise is simple: do good and be around to see others reap the benefits of your efforts. In fact, ensure you are there to help direct your giving. Be around to witness the beneficiaries of your charity getting the most benefit possible while you guide the application of your philanthropy. In the history of humanity, there may not have been a greater time than right now for those in need of charity. There has been such an accumulation of wealth (the drastic economic events of 2008 excluded) in the past ten to twenty years that giving it away seems the only way to distribute the massive fortunes some have made. In current times, there are plenty of philanthropic examples to follow.

Who are our great living philanthropists? What changed for them? I'm sure a number of contemporary icons come to mind. These are people who made conscious, living decisions to give. They had a vision for how their specific place in the world would help them give back, and they all leveraged their incredible energy, their money, their fame and success and friends to move their ideas forward. Besides having an overwhelming motivation to solve a problem or crisis or help a cause, they all shared a common understanding that was either inherent in their psyche or based in their religious or personal beliefs: doing good brings good things. Doing good, as these people have has brought them incredible abundance, admiration and wholeness in life that few people experience. They also show, in their diversity, that it is never too late or too early in life's stages to acquire this.

My list of contemporary icons is made mostly of people who were great to start with. These people had accomplished many things in their lives, which would traditionally define them as great successes. Some were in the music industry, others were from the business and investment world. One was an innovator who revolutionized technology, another was a retired and well-liked politician with scandals dogging him and another was a cultural and media sensation. Prior to their conscious decisions to effect change, they were well-known, successful and truly hadn't differentiated themselves that much from their peers. Gradually they became well-known for their accomplishments. They were leaders in their respective pursuits, but there were others who would and did rival them. They would be categorized with other great leaders in their fields. They would all make the decision to differentiate themselves at one point along the line, and for every one of them, that decision was personally motivated. After they made this choice to pursue intentional and strategic philanthropy, they advocated causes in need of support, inspired global movements and improved millions of lives. In some cases, they saved millions of lives. They moved ahead of their peers, out of the fray and into the light. These people went from being great to being iconic.

So here is my list of notable living philanthropic icons: Oprah Winfrey, Bob Geldof, Bono, Bill Clinton, Sir Richard Branson, Bill and Melinda Gates and their good friend Warren Buffett. Let's look at each of their transitions from great leader to iconic global philanthropist.

Let's look at one of the longest-standing philanthropic icons on my list first. He is a singer-songwriter born in 1951 and raised in Dun Laoghaire, Ireland, lead singer of the Boomtown Rats and actor on the iconic movie Pink Floyd The Wall. His mother died at the early age of forty-one, suffering from a brain hemorrhage. Robert "Bob" Frederick Zenon Geldof was on a typical trajectory shared by many charismatic rock stars.

Then, in 1984, something monumental had begun to occur, and for Geldof, what was taking place would change his life and the lives of millions forever. It was a drought—of historic proportions. A news report playing out on the BBC with images of thousands of helpless children starving had an immediate and profound impact on Geldof. He thought of his own beautiful one-year-old daughter, FifiTrixibelle Geldof, and the devastating implications of a biblical-sized famine. He was compelled to do something to help. One of the longest, most destructive droughts in African history, the Ethiopian famine, was rendering an entire nation helpless and wrought with cataclysmic starvation. Millions of people and children were going to die—that year if nothing was done to help. In fact, over one million people died of starvation during the Ethiopian famine in the early eighties. In 1984, Geldof recruited the help of Midge Ure of Ultravox and formed the group Band Aid to record, "Do They Know It's Christmas?", which became the biggest-selling charity single ever sold.

Maintaining his momentum, Geldof followed this massive hit and assembled the Live Aid concert, which was held on two continents simultaneously and is still revered as one of the most significant concert events ever, alongside the Woodstock Festival. The Live Aid concert, inspired and led by Geldof, raised over 150 million British pounds and it is estimated to have saved millions of lives. The former rocker and Boomtown Rats front man was knighted in 1986 and won the Beacon Fellowship Prize in 2005 for his leadership in alleviating poverty, famine and genocide in Third World countries and for advocating father's rights. Bob Geldof is a philanthropic icon.

I'll admit that in the late eighties and early nineties, Oprah Winfrey was not my favorite media personality. I'll also confirm that I was precisely not her target demographic, being a single white male eighteen to twenty-six years old living in Canada. I know that was a highly sought-after demographic, but it wasn't Oprah's. In fact, I found her typical talk-show format to be no more engaging than Phil Donahue's or Sally Jesse Raphael's. For those of you who recall those talk shows, that pretty much says it all. Oprah's rising stardom was predicated on a great work ethic, her charisma and a genuine connection with her mostly female viewers. Millions of women would tune in daily to hear what Oprah had to say, and husbands across North America would get an earful that evening. I know it's not the most politically correct thing to say, but it was certainly true.

Then, one day, that all changed. Well, perhaps it took more than just one day, but in a relatively short period of time, Oprah decided she would not be confined by the traditional fodder that her peer group was peddling and advertisers were paying significant sums for. She wanted every one of her programs to have meaning. She made specific efforts to change the types of guest she would have on her show and the actual meaning—or message—of each show itself.

After having been on television for years already, Oprah revolutionized TV talk shows in the period of 1994-1996. While she maintained her fan base, it took a while for others to become convinced that Oprah was serious and her ideas would catch on. You can just imagine the look on the faces of her publicists and television executives when she broke the news that she wanted every show to have a positive message. Advertisers were heavily funding controversy, drama and despair. Her intentions were not another marketing ploy. She was willing to go against the grain and fix challenging problems with her show instead of exploiting them, like her peers so often did.

Her movement to change the lives of Americans and millions of viewers worldwide by supporting and exploring the most fundamental societal needs took hold, and Oprah and her daytime show rose above all others. The focus of the shows became literacy, physical and mental health, preventing abuse, childhood and adult education and overall well-being. Her guests were experts on the subjects that held a measure of goodness, with values-driven topics, and there would be a positive message to be discovered in every show. Her show and media presence became a platform from which Oprah moved from being an industry leader to being iconic. Over the past ten to twelve years Oprah created the Angel Network, which has raised over $80 million and changed the lives of millions of people, and at the same time she became one of the richest woman in the U.S. with over $2.7 billion of personal financial worth[3]. She is easily one of the most influential and likely the most respected and recognized woman in the world. Oprah is a philanthropic icon.

If you want controversy and a little spice in your political leaders, Bill Clinton certainly fits the mould. While enjoying a tremendous rise to power in the White House, giving the Democrats a strong eight-year lock on the top job running the most powerful nation in the world, Clinton also enjoyed the luxuries of his powerful position as the head alpha male a little too much and a lot too indiscriminately. His philandering caught up with him in a very public way, and he ended his presidency in a disgraced manner while publicly shaking the foundation of his family.

Post-presidential life suited Clinton much better. In fact, after a couple of years out of office, he began to discover his true calling through philanthropy. He started a philanthropic family foundation, perhaps originally as a way to provide some tax relief from the high-revenue speaking engagements he had around the world. Somewhere along the way, Clinton started to take his role as philanthropist seriously and began to understand his significant global influence. Interestingly enough he had pulled his family back together again around the same time. He learned that he could use his expanding wealth to get projects off the ground, but better still, he could open doors pretty much anywhere in the world that needed to be opened to further a cause. Clinton has done just that. As a result of this realization and the recent years of action backing up his words, Bill Clinton has positioned himself as a global icon.

Sir Richard Branson has always raised his profile above the crowd. He is a bold and courageous adventurer, a brash and innovative business leader and has utilized his larger-than-life thinking and friendly contacts to become one of the world's most influential and recognizable philanthropists. He grew up in the U.K. in an upper middle class family, the eldest of four children. His grandfather was a judge in the High Court of Justice and a Privy Councilor. His father was a Barrister. Branson wasn't a particularly good student, and he suffered from dyslexia. While his academic prowess was less than outstanding, he excelled at sports. Branson's business legacy started in the early seventies with the launch of Virgin Records, and his entrepreneurialism grew and grew with Virgin becoming a ubiquitous brand, recognizable throughout the world.

Six years ago Branson launched Virgin Galactic—a company impelling the drive to commercial space travel. You would expect nothing less from a man who has circumnavigated the globe in a balloon and raced across the oceans and English Channel in a variety of marine vehicles. It would be safe to suggest that Branson has not been hindered by his dyslexia; neither did he have any particularly harrowing childhood trauma that might have shaped his philanthropy. Instead it was his tremendous success in life, his global awareness and respect for the good fortune and great responsibility that accompanied his immense self-made wealth that inspired him. His sense of the crisis of lacking leadership around the world compelled him to bring his leadership skills, enthusiasm and financial muscle as well as his personal friends—some of the most important personalities of the twentieth century—together to unify a movement that is charged with developing leadership. Strong moral leaders will teach and guide others to contribute to society and will share their knowledge and ideas. Great leaders will help build great nations. Sir Richard Branson will leave his mark as an icon.

Let's look at Bill and Melinda Gates and their relationship with Warren Buffett. While Warren Buffett is known as one of the savviest investors ever and one of the world's richest men, Bill and Melinda Gates will be forever known as the couple who convinced the greatest investor and world's richest man to loosen his hermetically sealed purse strings and invest his wealth with no direct financial return for the effort.

Bill Gates and Steve Jobs gave the world the personal computer. This computing revolution changed all our lives forever. They did a great thing for society in their business and as a result they became richer than most people in the world. As will happen with any revolutionary accomplishment, imitators and innovators rose as well. In fact, the up and comers rose above Gates' Microsoft in a lot of ways. Over time there was better technology, better software, problem-free operating systems and more exciting business propositions. While the PC brought profound change to the world, it also brought about imitators, copycats and innovators who quickly filled the space around Gates' company. Over time, it was the universality of the Microsoft platform that carved out a monstrous global market share. The reach of the business was endless. During Gates' last few years at the helm of Microsoft, his legacy was in personal computing innovation and his immense wealth, created by the meteoric rise of the company. He will definitely be remembered for this. His legacy will be stronger, for his incredible wealth, than those of most people on my list.

Always behind the scenes as Bill developed one of the most important companies of the twentieth century was Melinda Gates. She knew there was more to life outside the software development world they were living in. While Bill lived and breathed software, Melinda tried to create a sense of normalcy within the Gates family in an attempt to connect them with the world beyond Microsoft. In 1994 through 1996, Bill and Melinda formed the Bill & Melinda Gates Foundation. The mandate of the foundation was to improve global health and meet community needs.

It would be the vehicle through which they would direct their vast wealth in their efforts to change the world, starting in places where help was needed the most and resources were at a minimum. They would fund at the grassroots levels.

To date, they are the largest philanthropic benefactors in history with over $50 billion in assets and funding for beneficiaries worldwide[4]. This combined with Bill's influence on the giving decisions made by good friend Warren Buffett as well as a recent call to action for the billionaires of the U.S. to pledge as much as half of their wealth to charity over or after their lifetimes defines the Gateses as philanthropic heavyweights. Bill was a great innovator and with the help of Melinda was able to use long-term sustainable funding to create massive change in some of the world's most needy locations. Bill and Melinda Gates are now icons.

Next to Bob Geldof, Paul David Hewson, a.k.a. Bono, is a personal favorite of mine. I'm including Bono in this list because I believe he is really only just getting started. The lead singer of the influential band U2 grew up in Ballymun, a community in Dublin, Ireland. He grew up in the era of the IRA and as a young man witnessed the direct oppression that the religious-based political civil war imposed upon his community.

During the eighties, Bono and his band U2 ascended to incredible fame, and after the 1987 release of their biggest album ever, The Joshua Tree, they became one of the most influential music acts in the world. Their road to stardom didn't end there, and they released hit album after hit album, always innovating and impressing. Through his career Bono understood that his fame and influence through music could move people. He could effect change. By no coincidence, Bono was a key member of the Band Aid project led by Geldof. Bono's "ONE" campaign has enlisted the help of world leaders and other iconic figures such as Nelson Mandela, George W. Bush, former Prime Minister of Canada Paul Martin, and former U.S. Treasury Secretary Paul O'Neill.

Bono's causes—AIDS and Third World debt relief—have challenged world leaders to do better and resulted in billions of dollars being directed to Africa to fight AIDS and helped to lift African nations out of abject poverty. Bono has won many prestigious awards. He was named one of Time magazine's "100 Most Influential People" in 2004 and 2006 and shared Person of the Year honors with Bill and Melinda Gates in 2005. He was nominated for the Nobel Peace Prize in 2003, 2005 and 2006. In 2007 Bono was knighted and won the NAACP Image Award's Chairman's Award.

Bono has transitioned from rock star personality to truly great philanthropic icon. He has done this through his incredible personal connections with world leaders and his willingness to challenge them publicly. The true impact of his tireless efforts for AIDS, Africa and social change for our planet is likely yet to be realized.

Wow! That was inspiring, wasn't it? What defines those individuals is the fact that they acted. They intentionally initiated philanthropy. No more than that. They might not have been wealthier than you. Okay, maybe some like Buffet, Gates and Branson were, oh and Oprah too, but they didn't all start that way. They also might never have had the experience or responsibility of being in charge of a large organization or of having invented a new thing or system, but they acted on their ideas. They were consciously committed, tireless and shameless in their efforts.

You might feel somewhat overwhelmed or unprepared, and you might not feel up to the challenge. Then again, maybe you are moved to act. You might even wonder to yourself, what was so great about those people? You may feel you are even better positioned than they were to make an impact. Well, let's get busy and see if we can change your life! As you will notice, the common thread in the stories of our icons wasn't a business decision or some kind of ego-driven choice to become iconic; it was a decision to actually change the world, and each person applied their own unique skills, expertise and positions to the task. The decisions were bold and brash. These people often made choices that were unpopular (usually with their managers, publicists or hangers-on), sometimes risking the alienation of their fan base or at least pushing their supporters into uncomfortable territory. But after the initial shock of the transition wore off, their supporters became avid and outspoken advocates. Some even became inspired to devote themselves to their most important causes, themselves. It will take a bold step for you to truly change, but you are capable of it and you have likely done it before.

As in your business experience, the next steps you take are not random. Proceeding to make a deeper impact beyond a financial gift requires specific, diligent action. There needs to be a plan—although we all know this plan will constantly evolve—and people need to be involved who can help.

Let's look at things from 30,000 feet. We need to discuss philosophy, and motivation. What do you stand for? Why? What are your motivations in this process?

In the next chapter we will review the landscape of philanthropy and look at how we give, why we give and where and when we give. We will look at the demographics of giving and try to provide a clear view of the horizon you will be steering toward.

FUNDAMENTALS OF GIVING
Why Do We Give?

What motivates us to open up our hearts and wallets or volunteer our time? Studies have shown the number one reason that we give is that we have a feeling of compassion for those in need. Next to that, a personal cause will drive us to act along with a desire to give back to the community. If we were affected by a specific issue or cause or organization, we will seek to give support to that cause. For many of us, religious beliefs play a role in our motivations for giving. Financial reasons rank below those as motivations. In fact, according to the Statistics Canada Survey of Giving[5], Volunteering and Participating, conducted in 2004 and 2007, less than 23 percent of respondents stated that the income tax benefits of giving were the driving force behind their philanthropy.

What drives our icons to act? Well, Bob Geldof was overwhelmed with compassion when the extent of the crisis in Ethiopia became known to him. Oprah Winfrey's list of motivations is long, including her experience as an African-American girl growing up in inner-city Milwaukee and rural Tennessee, having been raped at the age of nine and becoming a mother at fourteen whose child died in his first weeks of life[6]. Her experiences gave her unique insights into the direct effects of illiteracy, child abuse and the absence of a family unit, as well as insights into the experiences of women, particularly African-American women, in poor communities in the U.S. Her personal experience and causes that touched her throughout her growth as a prominent woman in America were key motivations behind the many initiatives and philanthropic efforts she has spearheaded.

For Bill and Melinda Gates, a motivation might have been the gross inequity of Bill's success coupled with the massive social challenges he viewed that were faced around the world. His platform for philanthropy at the grassroots levels of education, health and medicine is focused on life's crucial needs, in contrast to his own success. Gates' motivation was to have an impact and to surpass what he had already achieved. He desired to redirect his immense wealth to life-changing, global projects. His passion moved Warren Buffett. When history looks back at Bill Gates, the philanthropist, the greatest impact his efforts had might have come through joining forces with the other richest man on the planet and funding lasting change. Bill and Melinda, through their friendship with Warren Buffett, were probably the only two people in the world with the ability to spur him to explore his philanthropic interests directly with his money. This from-the-top-down effect initiated by the Bill and Melinda Gates is one of a kind.

This is precisely what I am trying to do by highlighting the stories of global icons: I am trying to influence you from the top down. These people have leadership qualities and have raised themselves above the crowd. We all look up to them in some way. Their leadership is convincing since they are very successful individuals, many of whom came from rather moderate or even humble upbringings. There are thousands of inspiring philanthropists who are remarkable but who haven't the wealth or the social status of these icons. It is in human nature to view these people with admiration, but most leaders won't look to them for their business advice. Have you ever really followed the financial recommendations of someone lower on the ladder than yourself? Not usually. Understanding your influence and leadership position adds to your effectiveness as a philanthropist.

In contrast, Bono's personal experiences growing up exposed him directly to the unjustness of oppressive influences of governments on the people they govern. He opted to pick on the bully and stand up with a loud voice for others who were not able to do so for themselves. He gained an understanding that the oppressed can rise when given a chance. They can accomplish amazing things when they are unencumbered. At the outset, he had no practical experience or knowledge of the monetary system of the world and the international credit marketplace, but he knew that squeezing the already impoverished was a losing proposition. Not only could you not expect blood from a stone; it was possible the stone might be used to threaten or even kill you, if there were no other options. The expanding global travel and reach of U2 provided Bono with worldliness and a view of all different forms of commerce.

The cultural differences and clear socioeconomic separations within nations were very apparent to him. While western cultures have a spectrum of wealth distribution from the poor through the middle and upper classes, many Third World countries have just two divisions—the very rich and the very poor. What is clear in these societies is that the very rich have no interest in the poor achieving success and closing the gap. It is easier to keep people in line when they have no power or financial strength and rely upon the governing class for food, shelter and clothing. There is no choice for people in that financial condition. Generations are born into poverty, illiteracy and strife. Bono's experiences in Africa opened his eyes to this and he saw greatness in the people of Africa while they were being born into a life with no upside. It became Bono's mission to level the playing field, to free people from an inherently oppressive existence that, in turn, could give hope, provide opportunity and strengthen entire nations.

When reviewing these examples of some of our icons I want to reiterate why people give: it really is because they care. Giving comes from the heart. It is borne of personal experience and the human condition. It is not financially motivated. I have met many philanthropists who have stated that philanthropy was in their very nature, that it was part of the fabric of their being. For many, their earned and accumulated wealth unleashed this quality. Giving was natural; it was the way it should be. Wherever possible, through their lives they were able to lend a hand.

I know that each one of you reading this book is motivated to help and has likely already been giving throughout your life. No one has to tell you why you give. What I want to do is to inspire you and help you focus your giving in the most useful way possible, ensuring your effort is reaching the intended beneficiaries of that giving and our society as whole. The world will be a better place if more great people and leaders can become inspired to pursue philanthropy in their lives. Some of you might even become global icons. My goal in writing this is to inspire just one of you to reach those heights and dedicate your life to philanthropy.

In order to tackle a problem, we must first understand the landscape. We must carry out our form of intelligence gathering and market research. It is important for us to understand what the state of philanthropy and the non-profit world is now. North America is the most concentrated source of non-profit financial and volunteer support in the world. It is reasonable to expect that would be the case, due to the proportionately greater amount of wealth owned by the population in North America than in other countries throughout the world, along with an ongoing emphasis on spending more on leisure time in our western culture.

The charity and non-profit industry in the U.S. accounts for as much as 10 percent of all jobs and contributes close to 8 percent of all wages and salaries paid. It would be reasonable to assume that the culture of the people in the U.S. would not be very giving, as it is the most capitalistic society in the world —the premise of competition and individualism is pervasive, a rather eat-or-be-eaten mentality—yet there is something that goes beyond that for most Americans. It is the sense of community, a sense of unity and belonging. Lending a hand to others in need and giving back their considerable wealth to the community are also part of the culture of the U.S. Possibly it comes from the understanding that, by design, there are fewer social safety nets and it is everyone's responsibility to lend a hand so that the overall community thrives, thus supporting more growth and ultimately more success. This is the buy-in to a bargain that helps ensure there is fertile ground to grow the entrepreneurial spirit. It might seem to be the antithesis of capitalism, but maybe it's just capitalism with a social conscience.

In Canada, the non-profit sector represents roughly 6.8 percent of the GDP. There are 161,277 registered non-profit organizations and over 80,000 charities, representing over $171 billion in assets earmarked for their respective causes[7]. In the U.S. over 1.5 million non-profit organizations account for as much as 2.2 percent of the GDP and contribute over $700 billion to the economy, with over $300 billion being donated annually to charities by individuals, corporations and foundations[8].

Let's take a look at how we, as a society, give. There are a multitude of ways giving is carried out. I have summed them up in just a few broad categories. Volunteering, donating goods and services or cash, and sharing knowledge are our direct mechanisms of giving. Visible or vocal support lends itself to leading by example, while those viewing the participation of an influential person or company then further the cause on behalf of that person or by becoming a patron of the business. This form of extended giving is hard to quantify in terms of reach or measurable impact. Some forms of active patronage could be buying green products, boycotting corporations, or by providing support of high-profile causes. More formalized types of charitable involvement include voting as a shareholder on corporate issues or policy and investing in socially responsible businesses. These more structured types of activism are powerful because they become a part of our social consciousness and result in cultural movements or overall changes in behaviors.

In studying where and how giving is most prevalent, you will find that the reasons are linked to both the prosperity of a region and the general belief systems of that particular place. For example, if the demographic of a population in a given area is more religious, then giving per capita is reflected by that geographical concentration through greater philanthropic activity by members of a church, synagogue or mosque.

Additionally, you might find that there is more likelihood of giving to causes that mirror or support the basic beliefs of that specific religious group. In contrast, if there are communities in coastal areas where outdoor activities are characteristic of the population and where urbanization might be encroaching on nature, you could find a higher concentration of philanthropic efforts geared toward ecological preservation or in support of green living alternatives.

Throughout a culturally diverse nation, the motivations for giving will be as different as the people living there. A very interesting thing is the variety of intrinsic and external motivations for giving for the icons I have listed. They all have achieved so much, yet their personal motivations for giving are all quite different. That is reflected in the ways they give, ranging from affiliation to activism to mentoring to funding. Their methods of giving are possibly a result of their life experiences in their specific demographic region or culture, and are influenced by their past and also their present situations.

You could suggest that Sir Richard Branson's motivations and the direction of his attention are greatly influenced by his more current business experiences as well as his understanding of geographic and demographic idiosyncrasies. The same business influences could be stated for Bill Gates and Bill Clinton, though their giving manifests itself in many different ways. As for Oprah Winfrey, Bono and Bob Geldof, it is clear their past lives significantly shaped their current giving. But more often a common thread through philanthropic motivations would be childhood exposure to negative influencing forces, particularly unjust or oppressive forces, from politics to poverty, illiteracy and race, combined with the rise to the highest levels of power or success from such downtrodden or middle-class upbringings.

It is clear that philanthropy does stem from personal experience and a connection with one's surroundings. It is also apparent that the form of giving that is embraced is often connected to those experiences and surroundings that have shaped a person's life. Also, not often has the motivation for great philanthropy originated from the view of the top of the socioeconomic ladder, suggesting that affluence and entitlement aren't exactly great breeding grounds for philanthropic behavior. Rather, perhaps it is the struggle to achieve that status that is the motivator. The lifetime experiences of those who have built vast fortunes from humble beginnings tend to be very conducive to giving.

Naturally, the wealthy few have had some of the most historically significant impacts. It only takes one billionaire to provide the financial means and influence to equate with the financial efforts of thousands of people with less means. But one thing is clear: it is both the good and bad experiences accumulated over a lifetime that breed the humility and the instinct to give back. One ultra-wealthy philanthropist from Calgary once told me that while he was essentially "born" into philanthropy, he thought one of his greatest rewards for giving was the influence he had on his peers, who might otherwise have been less philanthropic, and their decision to give or act. His influence caused others to give large sums of money, thus financing research or initiating critical projects.

For many, giving is just a way of life. It is second nature to give to your church, to support local charities and to participate in charitable events. Lending a hand, making a donation and supporting the community are just things a person is expected do. They are a habitual behaviour. For others, their decision to give could stem from a personal crisis, or even a liquidity event for a business owner, unlocking new wealth. For me, my evolving philanthropy has been spurred by a desire to formalize the giving I have always done so that my efforts become much more effective. In some cases, philanthropy can be a product of estate planning, planned giving or a bequest. I have heard sophisticated tax and estate planners often cite their creation of a skillful planning process as a catalyst for giving, but that is a widely unfounded yet largely accepted belief.

The catalyst always lies within the individual, not the tax structure. It is the personal motivation that is strong enough to cause action. In my experience working with the wealthy and ultra-wealthy, I have found that they tend to act when they are good and ready. No financial adviser or tax planner will compel them to act. The final decision to move forward is always personal. There are many ways to save tax or preserve an estate. Charity doesn't always fall in line with a person's beliefs or desires and thus does not resonate with those who are not already predisposed to or pondering philanthropy. One thing the financial planning process can sometimes do is stimulate or reinforce the realization and assurance that the individual can actually afford to give. That is a fundamentally basic need for everyone: they need to know they will be able to care for themselves and their families as they had hoped and planned.

It is rare that financial benefit is the cause of philanthropy; quite often, financial benefit is a byproduct. When looking at the different points in time that the icons I have listed in this book made their decisions to embrace philanthropy completely, their wealth began to grow almost exponentially. It really is amazing. In financial planning circles there is often reference to a pyramid of personal success, reflecting Abraham Maslow's hierarchy of needs. The simple premise is that people will choose to give once they have provided for their personal financial security—their families' security and legacy—and ultimately then they are prepared to give, to explore their social capital. This is a tipping point, driven by a realization of financial security. This realization comes at different times for different people. A strong financial adviser or accountant can map out the likelihood of financial success and maybe bring this to the forefront of their clients' minds a little earlier than when their financial security is a foregone conclusion. This can put things in motion and lead to better and longer-term planning for philanthropic giving.

But I would like to expand on this and suggest something deeper and more established. I strongly believe that most people have an innate desire to give, and that they do so in many different ways throughout their lives. Giving is not only the act itself but a pursuit of identifying suitable ways to do so, along with a need for financial security. I see this as a parallel, not sequential, chain of events. The duality of this can be seen in the mode of giving, not through the gift itself.

The young give time and energy through volunteerism, activism and participation, the middle-aged give a combination of these, usually focused on family and friends and their immediate community, and the older, more financially secure provide financial funding to both local and far-reaching causes. Also they provide mentorship and leadership. But all groups make the same fundamental decisions to give. It is more than a desire to do so; it is a need to do so. It is our human inclination to be social, to be part of a socially connected community. While experiencing that connectedness, we seek ways to be needed, relied upon. For most of us, there is a tendency to derive our sense of self-worth from the eyes of those around us. We want to be useful in some way. It gives us great pleasure to provide solutions, comfort, guidance or support to those in our lives. It makes us feel good.

A powerful combination would be a direct pairing of those who have extraordinary energy and passion with those who have influence and money. This combination is embodied in our philanthropic icons. All of them had and have money and influence, although most of them were not as influential or wealthy before they embarked on their journey. Some of them were very wealthy, while others were just on the verge of this. In fact, I would suggest that the immense wealth some of them have experienced in their lives grew exponentially after they began concentrating on philanthropy.

Take Oprah, for one example. She was reasonably wealthy and famous in the mid-nineties when she consciously decided to direct every effort of hers to a common good. It was this bold step that elevated her status, broadened her audience and created a global awareness of her efforts. Another great example would be Bono and U2. They were a great Irish rock band living the rock and roll dream. They had huge western audiences. Their U.K. and North American fan bases were their meal ticket. Then, as Bono become more and more visible as the face of the struggle in Africa and as a supporter of freeing the impoverished from their debt and disease, U2 gained widespread global appeal and became one of the biggest global touring rock acts of all time. Its worldwide tours are now some of the most profitable acts in history. Last year the band grossed over $311 million[9]. This doesn't happen only because of great music; it is because the band has an impact on people. It can influence ideas and motivate behaviors. Fans want to listen to its music, but they also want to actively be a part of the positive efforts of Bono and U2.

Oftentimes, though, those most financially able to contribute are less inclined to drive a project, while those who would passionately pursue a cause are often unable to sustain their personal financial lives while doing so. Isn't that a conundrum? Add in the fact that there is a massive generational gap between those two groups and the powerful combination of drive and means is far too uncommon. So now I take the opportunity to promote the concept of mentoring as a meaningful alternative strategy to help those with the means finance those with the energy to get to the ends. All great leaders must view this as an extraordinary opportunity. We should cultivate giving at all stages of life and in all contexts possible.

Combining the financial wealth, the experience and knowledge of longtime community leaders with the passion, energy and open-mindedness of youth can make a powerful pairing. Each can learn from the other, and in fact that is how these matches are often portrayed—as a great opportunity for the elders to teach the young ones the wisdom they've accumulated and, in doing so, perhaps have a little trendiness rub off on them from the youth.

You might easily contend that it would serve just as well for the two groups to focus on applying their strongest attributes and collaborating to solve an issue or direct change. The learning from each other and the mutual benefits would flow naturally, but with the focus on the task at hand and their attention on the challenge they would be able to direct their efforts on progress rather than on what they intend to gain from working together. Too often the premise of the mentoring process is to gain something, while a huge opportunity of bringing a powerful combination of divergent skills to the table might be missed. The relationship is between the mentor and the mentored instead of between the pair and the beneficiary.

Is Philanthropy A Conscious Decision?

No one decides to become a philanthropist. But they do decide to commit to give back in some way and make all their actions count, thus becoming philanthropic. This is a very conscious step. It is a radical and courageous decision to break away from what is expected of you in your profession and change your daily business, or to apply your effort to focus solely on social returns as the end result, with profit becoming a byproduct of your focus and not the goal.

This is the essence of the stories of philanthropic icons in this book — the transition from being a charitable or generous person to being a true philanthropist who makes giving the focus of their life and makes the goal of their business to create a social profit. All outcomes are then intended to be for good — to do good, as it were. This next level of thinking or behavior is fundamental to any successful pursuit. You will find that strong values-based organizations rise to the top of the chain of success.

While Google is not a charity, and its massive and extremely profitable advertising revenue model would not be considered a byproduct of charity by many, you have to understand that the company does stand for doing the right thing. It has values that are deeply ingrained in its attitudes and culture. Some of Google's ten corporate philosophies highlight that doing the right thing will result in good things happening to you. A key tenet would be that "you can make money without doing evil." [10] Google is a principles-based entity. It has had unprecedented success for many reasons, but underlying them all, I believe that the fundamental principal of having good intentions is most important. Just review Google's latest scuffle with China over censorship of its website searches and you will see a company that opted to choose values-based philosophical beliefs over its bottom line. I believe that practices such as that will drive and expand Google's fortunes for years to come.

In contrast, have a look at Facebook's recent challenges and the claims against it, which state that it was established purely to gather critically important personal information about its users that would be vital to a more advanced and focused effort to sell them products and services. While this might have been apparent all along, Facebook never owned up to it. In fact, it appears to have been a subversive tactic that was shrouded in the friendly social connections Facebook was promoting. If the company does not make significant changes to the manner in which it behaves, socially, I feel that the growth of the business will falter on the shallow foundation it is based on.

Generally, the result of extraordinary dedication to one's craft, business or other activity based on a foundation of doing the right thing is lasting success. The same can be said of philanthropy. The fundamental premise is to do good; the next step is to support the intention with a quality business model. It is also likely that there is merit to the idea, for businesses having a long history of charitable involvement, that a great business model is the basis for taking the next step to greater fortunes.

On a more personalized note, the impact of a focused individual who understands how to move people to act for the benefit of a larger goal is an extraordinary thing. Once the individual begins to measure their impact in less obviously quantifiable terms, they begin to remove limits on what they hope to achieve. Their business model becomes open-ended. Their ultimate mission becomes true philanthropy.

STRATEGIC GIVING
Creating a Social Enterprise

Once a decision is made to pursue philanthropy by living the principle of doing good, we must look at outcomes. While we are well-intentioned and our motives are pure, we cannot embrace our target cause without understanding what the most effective outcome of our efforts would be. I would refer to this as applied giving—the actual implementation of your decision to become philanthropic. As with business, there are ways to succeed and there are most definitely ways to fail, even while your aim is to do the right thing.

Consider the over funded organization with no people or unqualified people to do the work. At first you might think this is inaccurate—that the organization is understaffed rather than over funded. I suggest over funded because the organization with the wrong people or unqualified staff at the helm creates as much a waste as one with less money and less talent. The efforts of these organizations will stall, and the funds will not effectively be put to work. And then there is the reverse—an organization that's overstaffed and under funded, with a lot of good intentions, stalled again on the factory floor. Research and development-heavy causes, such as cure-finding or development of treatment-based technologies, think tanks or policy lobby groups, etc., can be financially draining with significant staff requirements, but the possibility of failure carries enormous financial risk. Coming to grips with a lot of money spent for an ineffective solution while other simple causes go unfunded strikes a chord with everyone who is in the care of the public's trust and a beneficiary's hopes.

Let's look at the intersection between business and charity. Recently this has been referred to as social enterprise. It has often become a dead-end road, as businesses try too hard to impress their values on the social enterprise with the goal of generating a profitable bottom line. The social benefit goal with a profit guideline as a compass for direction does not always navigate a net return in the same way—in fact, the return on investment is largely not even quantifiable. This can often become the battleground between the board of directors (working for the funders—shareholders) of an organization and the executive staff of an organization (working for the beneficiaries). While both parties have the same ultimate goals, there is a great division on efforts and vantage points. In most cases their viewpoints could not be more different. Reconciling a return on investment (profit) with the social return on investment (impact) is challenging. In a for-profit business, the board represents the interests of shareholders, and the beneficiaries of the business enterprise are most often the shareholders, too. This alignment of interests in business is almost always present.

In the non-profit environment, the divergence of donor and beneficiary outcomes is where the crossroads of cash profit versus social benefit is located. Thus a focused effort is required by the board and the executive staff of the organization to steer the policies of the organization toward its stated mandate and direct the measurement of success to the outcomes circling around those targets. The mandate should direct the donors' attention to the beneficiaries' successes and thus help to provide better means by which success can be quantified. There are ways to successfully achieve this when compromise is reached.

It is also critical to understand the composition of the executive staff in a non-profit organization. The board of directors in most non-profits is typically made up of motivated, passionate individuals with a keen sense of their social responsibilities and some formal education in their field. You have to understand that a socially driven educational background is more often of the social, psychological or scientific nature and not derived from business schools, economics labs or finance faculties. This is something to be celebrated.

These leaders truly understand what their business is. Directors and advisers are often looked up to for the acumen they bring to the table, which is entirely different from the expertise of those who run the organization. To serve the beneficiaries on a day-to-day basis requires a very specialized skill set. In a large number of organizations, there is an enormous chasm revealed when the focus shifts from the ultimate mandate of the organization to the operational decisions and strategic planning. Executives are accustomed to solving problems immediately and putting out fires daily, while long-term preparation can be difficult to execute with pressing daily distractions. Coming from a very different viewpoint, the board will have a very different idea of how the organization should be run. There is both great opportunity as well as challenge in this.

Other types of organizational struggle for non-profits include the effort to turn good management into solid results. A great cause with strong funding but poor management, poor planning and ultimately poor productivity will result in goals not being achieved. Two possible results of a lack of management are obvious: 1) the creation of an inefficient entity —overwhelming cause being attacked by underwhelming organization, 2) the making of inevitable bad decisions—the management has its own agenda, such as earning a cushy salary without concern for beneficiaries or taking advantage of possibly nefarious tax breaks (such as charity drug tax-break schemes) or even become predatory or victimized (for example, the crushing effects of the over reliance on Bernard Madoff's investment scheme to manage large portions of capital for charitable organizations left charities victimized, but clearly there was mismanagement in terms of financial prudence and investment risk review).

Most charities operate extremely efficiently, achieving the biggest possible bang for their buck. High levels of volunteerism, stingy budgets and in-kind donations of goods and services increase the efficiency of organizations. For the organization's board and executives, it is critical to create a solid long-term plan, understanding the strengths of the organization and finding the best people to implement the plan. Maximizing and understanding the benefits of the social enterprise infrastructure can be very helpful.

As for getting the most out of personnel, the solution is to create the role first and then find the most suitable people to fill it. Avoiding development of positions around certain people is crucial. Roles are revealed by the mandate of the organization, as with any business. These are basic company building strategies that come into play. When looking at how you personally can have the most significant impact, review the best application of your skills, in the roles required by the organization and endeavor to surround yourself with the best candidates for every role.

The icons mentioned in this book have a clear understanding of their role and how they fit into their place within the organizations they support. Just look at Bill Gates. He has money and influence and the largest software development firm in world. His goal to fund and provide health and education on a worldwide scale is a perfect fit with his grasp of technology and interconnectivity.

Sir Richard Branson has extensive global personal networks, business contacts and an adventurous spirit. His peer group of business leaders, political figures and entertainment personalities is a huge advantage for executing high-level thinking and working to support grassroots movements from the top of the ladder. The people he influences can remove the obstacles in his path.

Bill Clinton clearly has significant political influence to go along with his charismatic demeanor. Additionally, the funds generated from his appearance fees have been significant and fund his efforts. His role is to highlight a cause publicly while making inroads through back room diplomacy.

Clearly Oprah Winfrey's media presence and personality are her strongest mechanisms for supporting social initiatives such as Oprah's Book Club, the Angel Network or informative programming (Dr. Phil, the Dr. Oz Show, shows on fitness and health, improving diet and nutrition, etc.). Oprah gets it. She understands that her skill is to place issues and supporters of causes into the public domain and to highlight their needs. She can use her own money as a source of funding, but she can also use her financial clout as a way to encourage advertising support for projects that might never be done otherwise. Her affiliation with them, can provide a strong profit for those who support them. Just look at those guests who have been on her show regularly. Where in the history of television talk shows has a regular appearance by one or more physicians to discuss everything from heart attacks to hemorrhoids been the launching pad for a television series focused on health issues and medical problems? Sponsors and advertisers understand the influence of Oprah, but Oprah, herself, has a much greater sense of this and the responsibility of her role.

Both Bob Geldof and Bono, as international music artists, can use concert events to raise awareness and significant funding, while their music transcends cultural and socioeconomic differences globally. Their roles as rock stars and philanthropists are clear. They understand they are allowed certain liberties that others might not be. Their audacity and outspokenness are their tools to get their message across. Their celebrity status gives them unprecedented access to world leaders, while their unabashed style allows them to get into the faces of those leaders and publicly challenge them. This image is part of their rock star persona and is expected. They can challenge the status quo and raise controversy, and this can broadcast a message to a broad audience and garner headlines that others might not be able to. Controversy is part of their role, and they both understand this very well.

An Inspired Process:
Transitioning From Great Leader to Great Philanthropist

The conscious decision to give, to apply all efforts toward a positive outcome, is a step forward in becoming a philanthropist. Your position of leadership and influence can make you an incredibly powerful resource. The application of your business savvy to a problem or project can create and innovate ways to solve problems. Defining the "profit" motive will blend social impact with financial outcomes. Let's discuss the intersection of business and social enterprise to highlight the significant congruencies and some differences that can be overcome or must be adapted to.

Business projects begin with the vision of an innovator and a guiding mission statement. They are outlined by a business plan, and the ultimate goal of business is to make a profit. Non-profit organizations also have a mandate or mission and sometimes a formal business plan and investment policy statement. They have the ultimate goal of affecting social change (providing a social return on investment). Both organizations have structures with board members, committees, executives, etc. Stakeholders in both types of entities range from shareholders/donors to employees/ volunteers, board members, customers/beneficiaries, community members, etc.

The key differences are few but quite distinct. In the business world, capital is easy to attract as the provider of the capital, through debt or equity, is seeking a presupposed return on their investment. There is a clear economic relationship between risk and reward—this is considered the deemed cost of capital. In the non-profit world, this relationship is less clear. Capital is received sporadically, typically in unpredictable quantities and from a variety of sources, from public funding to the private sector, from capital campaigns to planned gifts and seasonal giving. Typically, the donor gains an intrinsic reward for the mere act of giving and expects very little in return—in the form of some kind of noticeable impact within society. Donors do not expect any liquidity or financial return on their investment. While the actual financial gain is no more than the taxable benefit, the net tangible gain is next to nil. While on the donor side of the equation, the cost seems very high—or rather the return on capital seems quite low—the cost of capital to the organization appears to be very low in charity.

So the question that arises is what is the economic relationship? Does a low cost of capital suggest a low overall return? In investing this would imply safety, the lower the risk of the asset means less expected investment return. But for the donor, how is there "safety" of invested capital when there is no direct or often any measurable return? So does applying that model of economic evaluation to a donation or investment in charity actually work? Implying that there is a clear economic relationship related to cost of capital in a charitable environment would require a clear measure of investment, outcome and expected return. The intangibles in the measurement would be the answer, but this is something that has been a struggle for a large number of organizations to quantify.

In the realm of business, the economic upside of enterprise is financial gain. Those who want to use their expertise are rewarded with income that pays their bills, supports their families and is a key component of building multigenerational wealth. Most often, the promise of financial gain attracts those with more talent and broader business knowledge and expertise more than social ventures. There is a divide between the for-profit sector and non-profit sector when it comes to the executive talent pool. In some ways, this gap is filled by the extraordinary passion most in the non-profit sector bring to their roles every day. Volunteers comprise a large part of the staff that works in any social enterprise. These people have a desire to work and do not rely on the organization for their income, thus, in theory, improving the productivity of these organizations over those with employees, who might rather be working elsewhere but need the work to pay their bills. Imagine, as a business leader, having your organization supported by employees who are motivated purely by success?

The application of highly qualified business talent to social enterprise can deliver amazing results, but only if there is a common understanding of the purpose of the enterprise. It is important to take lessons from the impassioned as they inspire, encourage and motivate through example. Becoming passionate will play a key role in building an unwavering resolve to tackle challenges that only the non-profit sector can. There is prosperity in giving and one should embrace the step.

Enter into a social venture with the same drive and passion you would give to a for-profit enterprise, and there will be results. Understand the subtle differences for their strengths and you will quickly adapt. Profit and social impact can both be achieved, donors and shareholders are one and the same and volunteers bring as much or more to the table as paid employees. Non-profit organizations require more structured governance, financial management and stakeholder communication. Treat beneficiaries and donors as you would your shareholders; be accountable to them, be available to them and be transparent with them.

Accountability in business and social enterprise is vital to progress. Keeping an organization and the people working there accountable to a goal can be achieved in many ways. In business, the bottom line profit is a key driver, with employees always being aware or being reminded of their impact on that bottom line. Their performance is measured by their contribution, and their ongoing employment relies on it. In a social enterprise the measure can literally be the lives of the beneficiaries. An employee or volunteer will either be acutely aware of this or very far removed from the actuality of it. This really provides some mixed results.

For example, the cook who prepares food for Meals on Wheels might have no direct link to those they feed, and thus they might get the sense they are accountable only for the quota of food prepared. Conversely, the driver that delivers the meals each day knows exactly the impact and the gravity of their responsibility. Their accountability is very much linked to the beneficiaries, and lives might be at stake if they do not perform their role. Clearly, this level of accountability is profound. In business environments, achieving the minimum expected standard is how one is measured against expectations, and thus when a job is done, there is limited additional accountability to the organization. Meanwhile, in social enterprise, there is an ongoing sense of responsibility to the beneficiaries that drives action. There is a connectedness to the cause that borders on dependency. And when the beneficiary's needs have been satisfied momentarily, the current and future donors expect more.

Your Experiences
The Motivations for Your Inspiration

Sergey Brin, one of the founders of Google, once said that his biggest mistake in philanthropy was starting a charitable foundation. His experience suggested that it was best to create a social enterprise, make philanthropy the business, hire the best executives and run a 'profitable' charity. Through Google.org he has made efforts to pursue this strategy by investing in and encouraging businesses to innovate to solve major environmental issues of the planet, such as energy conservation, alternative fuels and the global climate. I strongly believe this is the best approach to most social challenges—that a blend of business acumen, innovation and strategy combined with a social goal can create very powerful solutions to some of the world's most difficult problems. Making the success of business and directing the efforts of the business to build enterprise with a social impact that, through its execution and efficiencies, creates a financial profit alongside a social benefit is something to aspire to.

The following describes how some iconic philanthropists identified their causes and applied their talents and strengths to finding solutions. You can see that some solutions are quantifiable in funds raised and problems solved immediately, while others will have profound multigenerational effects as the successes of this generation trickle down through the next and so on. Understanding how your strengths relate to a solution for the cause that is most important to you is the key to building your social venture.

There are actually some very consistent stages of philanthropic involvement, and they can be summarized as experiences which form motivation and provide cause affiliation, strength identification, strategy development and action, and finally reflection and refinement of effort. The philanthropist must clearly identify with and be inspired by a need or a cause to be most effective. This motivation will manifest itself as the individual discovers the best way possible in which they can support the cause or impart change. Strengths are called upon as organizational roles become established. For some, a simple acknowledgement that there is a need for fundraising would provide individuals, with the knack for convincing others, a way of sharing the worthwhile nature of the cause. If a person's strengths lie in marketing or public relations, their talents are quickly allocated to that effort. The next stage that follows the identification of one's strengths and how they fit within an organization is the development of a strategy to maximize the efforts put forth, and how to capitalize on success in keeping with the key strengths you bring to the table.

The icons we reviewed for this book all have very specific talents or strengths that they leveraged to gain the largest impact for their specific cause. For example, musicians Bono and Bob Geldof used the global reach of their music and the access it gave them to extend their voices. Geldof identified the cause that mattered most to him. He understood his influence through music and celebrity and used that to approach solutions to his causes in a rather innovative manner. Through the assembly of Band Aid for the recording of the hit song "Do They Know It's Christmas?" and the follow-up with Live Aid, the world's first and largest two-continent concert, Geldof was able to raise and direct millions of dollars directly to stop or prevent massive starvation in Africa. For Bono, in supporting the fight against AIDS and the reduction of the crushing effects of Third World debt, he knew that his notoriety and cocksure attitude could provide him with the right combination of access through stardom, support through musical following and political persuasion as he pushed through doors that would otherwise be closed to most people. He used this high-profile attention time and time again to put leaders on the spot, encouraging them to commit to the will of the moment and do what was right—to make promises to act that were so big they had to follow through or risk political consequences. This pressure on the leaders has caused them to free up millions in overwhelming debt payments, drew global attention to the AIDS epidemic in Africa and brought funding and medicine to the cause that would rank low in priority and public appeal had it not been thrust onto leaders in such a brash and public manner.

As a masterful politician and former President of the U.S., Bill Clinton understood he could gain the attention of millions when he spoke. His position could open discussion and provide political entry to sensitive areas most people don't even know exist. Clinton's goals of health security, economic empowerment, leadership development and citizen service as well as racial, ethnic and religious reconciliation meshed very well with his political influence, money and personal connections. In order to provide the solutions to his causes, he founded CGI—Clinton Global Initiative—to spur global leaders to meet and propose solutions for global problems. The enterprise was funded largely by the William J. Clinton Foundation, which was created in part to manage revenue from his financially lucrative public speaking events, as well as to accommodate outside donations that he generated through speaking for his causes. Through the application of his financial strengths and his ability to influence and access the highest levels of government, he was able to instigate government action, guide and push policy developments and spur the initiation of many projects worldwide aimed at furthering his goals to improve the world through solving some of the most fundamental challenges of race, financial disparity and health.

Business and media moguls Sir Richard Branson and Oprah Winfrey capitalized on their massive media appeal and charismatic charm to further their respective causes.

At the root of things, Oprah's motivations to give were the basic struggles of children in the environments of poverty and abuse. She knew her strengths, she knew her audience and she understood the power of her position. And so she targeted the very heart of the problem and directed her initial attention to improving literacy and using her platform to educate on abuse and health. The result of this focus was the establishment of the Angel Network and Oprah's Book Club as well as specialized programming designed to explore, explain and educate on abuse and family dynamics. The impact was massive. Oprah has raised tens of millions through her Angel Network and has inspired millions through her book club to pick up books and increase their literacy. The social awareness generated by her has a lasting impact on Americans, the effects of which will be seen through generations.

For Sir Richard Branson, his serial entrepreneurship and serial risk taking positioned him as a business icon as well as an exciting hero for the adventure-seeker in everyone. A common theme of Branson's exploits and pursuits is that of "innocent" fun (although it would be obvious to say daring and cheeky as well) and living life to its fullest. The combination of his energy and success has provided Branson with a global audience and respect. Being well-versed in the world made Branson's philanthropic eyes aware of the need for true global leadership. His cause, if you will, is to lead from the top down—to train and gather leaders of the world to unite in their efforts to be better people, to guide others to be better and to work together to solve the world's problems. His celebrity, business and political contacts allowed him to create his leadership group, called the Elders, to resolve conflicts and highlight solutions with a goal to relieve human suffering as well as support new business and economic development in impoverished areas. The Elders brings together leaders such as Archbishop Desmond Tutu and Nelson Mandela. It has been funded by Branson and his friend Peter Gabriel.

These efforts have resulted in the dedication of world leaders to direct humanitarian projects and support grassroots initiatives to solve the challenges of basic human suffering in impoverished regions of the globe.

Finally, no one will shape the financial outcome of fundraising in the twenty-first century more than Bill Gates. Once the world's richest man and definitely in the top few for the past decade, Bill Gates has developed a deep understanding of his motivations for giving and an even more precise understanding of how his key strength could be used in furthering his cause. Inspired by a profound but simple motivation, Gates has applied his number one resource—his money—to improving the health of the world—which encompasses education, literacy, medical health, fighting disease and poverty, etc. By attacking the root problems in the world, Gates believes he will be able to improve the overall health of the world.

Of anyone, Gates has the money to do this. But as I said, he also understood his key strength, and that was not just his money, but also the money of his friends—who, of course, were the other richest people in the world. You could say that Bill Gates' main influence has been through his vast technological networks, his amazing resources for education, communication and innovation, but greater still, he was able to convince the world's most successful capitalists to part with their money in support of not-for-profit causes. Not only has he given his own money, but he also got Warren Buffett to pledge a portion of his enormous wealth to the Bill & Melinda Gates Foundation. To date, Warren Buffett has contributed over $6.4 billion, as well as an additional $2 billion gift announced in July 2010. The foundation gives over $3 billion each year to its various causes, focused on world health.

Bill and Melinda have also decided that they should team up with Warren Buffett in an unprecedented effort to have every billionaire in the U.S. pledge at least half of their wealth to charity during or at the end of their lifetime. This effort could create the largest source of non-profit funding the world has ever seen. They have called this the Giving Pledge and announced the first forty billionaires who had pledged part of their fortunes in a press release on August 4, 2010. You can read the actual written pledges of these people at *www.givingpledge.org*. These individuals and families represent some of the most high-powered and successful people on the planet. The list of those who have already pledged includes Michael Bloomberg, Larry Ellison, Paul Allen, George Lucas, Barron Hilton, T. Boone Pickens and Ted Turner, to name a few very high-profile billionaires. This monumental challenge to the richest people in the U.S. could generate a historic transfer of wealth from private citizens to the public philanthropic trust. With an estimated 400-plus billionaires in the U.S., this effort could theoretically bring over $1 trillion to the charitable sector.

It is conceivable that this formal challenge to the wealthiest among us could easily motivate others across the globe. While those with the most riches will be inspired to give through the influence of their peers, the trickle-down effect will also add fuel to the movement. While I have heard some commentary that states this will actually diminish the future giving of less wealthy individuals, I would suggest that the opposite will be true. If you were to ask the little old lady who attends church every Sunday and leaves her five dollars in the collection plate if she ever considered her gift to be insignificant when the church has billions of dollars worldwide at its disposal, I can assure you she will respond that she feels a responsibility to give and that she gains personal satisfaction from the act.

If you take a big-picture view of all this, in fact, it is likely that this could be the dawning of one of the most productive times in history for social enterprise. It is also quite apparent that the billionaire benefactors will not have a desire to give their money away to merely any organization without a plan, goal or infrastructure. This Giving Pledge will force non-profit organizations across North America to fine-tune their business plans, improve their governance and apply higher-quality fiduciary practices to their operations. There will also very likely be a shift to push businesses to become more philanthropic and for charities to become more businesslike. In the end, this will drive innovation and growth. By launching this initiative, Bill and Melinda Gates along with Warren Buffett have shown that they know where their strengths lie.

As you can see, there is vision that stems from leaders who choose a path of philanthropy. The point I have been trying to make is that these icons understood their motivations, which led them to their causes. They were able to take inventory of the strengths that made them most successful and could further their causes in the most effective way. With an understanding of personal motivation and strength, they applied their energy and effort to their causes. The results were solutions or organizations designed and created to solve specific problems. The results have been staggering so far. To think that just a handful of people have made such a huge impact. These contemporary icons have forged new paths, brought us together and led us to give.

Could you make that transition from casual observer to committed giver? What effect would it have if these leaders were the minority? What if twice as many leaders stepped up? What if another handful of multimillionaires or billionaires took on the next phase of philanthropy? How powerful of an impact could that have? Are you one of them? What makes these icons any better than you? They are not necessarily richer than you, nor are they any more innovative than you. They might not even employ as many people or generate the same revenue as you do, but they have assembled the right combination of steps. Just as a great golfer makes their swing look effortless while driving a ball 300 yards, our icons figured out the right application of force in the right sequence and had tremendous success in execution. You could probably match their impact; you just need to learn the sequence. Get your swing in sync. Imagine the change that would be possible if there were more people with such money, influence and passion, like our icons, applying their strengths to improve the world.

Motivation

While we have touched on some of the rationales for the involvement of our icons in their causes, yours might be entirely different. Interviewing a wide range of philanthropists, social activists and business leaders for this book, I found a myriad of motivations that served to drive people to give. Motivations included a person being born into a circumstance, such as a disability or disease. Then, navigating through life's challenges as anyone would, they at some point started helping others in the same predicament or working to clear a path to ease a specific challenge encountered daily by someone they empathize with. These are people who are not only affected activists, but they stand out from their peer group in that they have made the conscious decision to act.

Some others were affected through their personal relationships; a parent, spouse, child or friend's experience had motivated them to become involved, be it for the sole purpose to help the ones they loved or to facilitate improvements for those who might be impacted in future generations. Along the same lines, there were cases of mentors who had dedicated their lives to helping others and whose influence caused the individual to follow in their footsteps, taking up their cause. Others had been drawn to the profession of giving and chose charitable work as a career path, evolving into the philanthropist they are today as they found a passion for their work.

A common thread for these people, though, was that philanthropy evolved—from involvement and circumstance to commitment and passion. Those who would be considered true philanthropists are characterized by living a life of giving that has become part of their very being. It reminds me of a saying that I enjoy, about the difference between the chicken and the pig in your Sunday morning eggs and bacon breakfast. The chicken was merely involved in the process, but the pig was truly committed. I'll admit that the thought of a pig is not really the most desirable connotation for us, but it is certainly a meaningful analogy. To be as committed as that little piggy was is critical. That pig was part of the very fabric of your breakfast. Your philanthropy must be the same; you must get some skin in the game.

I believe that motivation leads to involvement and involvement leads to commitment. Philanthropy is commitment. In every possible way, philanthropy is more the act than the thought.

One thing about motivation is that it stems from staring down our biggest fears and tackling them head on. Motivations can be a desire to avoid a circumstance, to prevent one or to better one that exists already. For our icons, their motivations can be witnessed through the vulnerability they exhibit as they share their passion for the causes they support. They have shared their challenges and triumphs with the world, in full view of everyone. Their egos have been heavily tempered with humility. Although most of us would believe otherwise—that these personalities are strong, dominant people with no sense of their weaknesses—I believe the case is very much the opposite. They clearly understand their weaknesses and they allow their compassion to guide them. It is the vulnerability in those leaders that draws us into their cause—not just their charisma or their strengths. We feel connected to their struggles, and we feel compelled to help as they help others. We trust their intentions and join in. To engage and to foster trust, you must exhibit your vulnerability.

Bob Geldof was deeply moved by the television images he viewed of helpless gaunt children starving en masse. They had no choice in the matter—it was their fate. The historic drought sapped a whole nation of its will and threatened an entire generation. Looking into the eyes of his one-year-old daughter, he saw a commonality of spirit, of helplessness and fragility. His gut response was heartfelt, as if it were his child he was seeing on the screen, starving to death. That motivation and the personal connection was enough to set a monumental project in motion. The Band Aid project was what Geldof envisioned as his small effort to make a difference. Through the lyrics and the song, his passion was conveyed to the world. Little did he know the combination of a great song and a timely ensemble of great relevant talent would send sales skyrocketing and finance a movement that led to Live Aid and the rescue of, literally, millions of starving Ethiopians. This feat would create tremendous opportunity for an entire generation of people that were almost robbed of their future by starvation.

Oprah Winfrey has also been intrinsically motivated by the struggles of children. Her own personal experiences of molestation and abuse growing up as a young child left indelible marks on her soul. She was raised by her grandmother on a small farm in Mississippi. At age six she moved into her mother's home in Milwaukee. The suffering of African-American children born into poverty and illiteracy that she both experienced and witnessed motivated her to begin her crusade to change the lives of millions through protecting, educating and nurturing the lives of children and their mothers. Her motivation was inspired by personal experience and observation.

Bono had grown up in the north Dublin suburbs during some of the most politically charged and religiously divided times in Europe in the last 100 years. The son of a Catholic father and Protestant mother, Bono had negative experiences in both Catholic and Protestant schools and struggled at home, immensely, upon the death of his mother. He was an unwilling participant in the culturally oppressive environment of that period. These events, coupled with the daily experiences living among the struggles of an entrenched sectarian society, motivated Bono to work to right the injustices he saw, thumb his nose at the oppressors and urge the masses to settle their differences and find a collective solution and harmony. This has always been evidenced in his music and is plain to see in his philanthropy. Bono challenges those in authority to do more, to help those who are unjustly caught in a larger struggle. His insolence and irreverence turns some people off. He campaigns to bring people together to solve some of our most unsavory difficulties, from AIDS and poverty to politically charged hotbeds dealing with powerhouse nations vying for control of their resources or geography. Bono has motivation burning from within. His is a controlled rage for peace and equality.

What is your motivation? What are your life experiences that inspire you to act? We all have our reasons to act. To share a little of my own story with you, I would say I have plenty of experiences that could provide the motivation for me to help a specific cause. I had a great childhood. There was a lot of love in my household and family, and I had a good education, excelled in many sports and music and had strong community ties and great friends. By all accounts I had a good upbringing, great health and would be considered reasonably successful in pretty much all parts of my life. That said, I lived in a particularly low-income neighborhood, with drug dealers, bike gangs and small-time thieves residing and carrying out their daily business activities around us. There was a family of at least ten Canadian Metis living in a tiny run-down home across the street. They were living off government subsidies and they pretty much lived in squalor, in an environment of alcohol abuse. In retrospect, a lot of my grade school mates didn't have things so good at home. There were quite a few broken homes and, looking back now, I think that there was probably some abuse in a small number of those homes. I could be motivated by those experiences to help find solutions for urban poverty and misled youth and abuse.

Or the fact that my father had suffered from schizophrenia since his late teens might be motivation enough. He struggled with the disease his whole life and I never really comprehended it until my adult years. I never knew him as being any different than the man he is and, by any standard for those gripped by schizophrenia; he is a success story. He is a particularly bright and kind man, and he had held many decent working positions. He worked hard to educate and train himself, functioned daily and even ran his own small business for a decade. While I later found out that he pretty much faked it a lot at work and would have really preferred being at home in bed hiding from the world most days, I never knew him or thought of him to be anything but a productive member of society and a decent provider for our family. Maybe I should be more in tune with the challenges of mental health and more motivated to support all the critical needs that go with them. I never felt affected, but I saw some of the suffering through my dad. He never lived up to his own expectations, but I certainly believe he far exceeded anything anyone could have possibly expected of him. He was a success, a good man, a loving father and doting grandfather. His experiences, though, pale in comparison to the suffering of millions who are profoundly affected daily by mental illness.

My mother had barely achieved her high school diploma (mostly due to falling in love with my father and caring for him during his early years gripped by mental illness). I suppose her efforts to always work hard and tirelessly improve herself as well as support my dad in keeping his sanity, all the while ensuring my sister and I continued living a normal childhood, could push me to help women struggling in the same circumstances. But my mother never asked for help. She stuck with my dad in the darkest times and through the nuttiest ones—and believe me, there were a few of those. She is, by all accounts, one of the most amazing women I have ever met. Her resolve to stand by her man and support him through everything, while living a life somewhat restricted by their circumstances, never once deterred her spirit. She is a sparkling light of optimism. She is a great woman, sincere friend and one of the most genuinely selfless people I have ever met.

I don't think I could actually pinpoint any of those experiences as the motivation for my interest in giving and becoming philanthropic. It's strange that this is the case. I would suggest that maybe it is more due to the fact that I feel so fortunate to have come out the other end of my childhood surroundings rather unscathed. I would guess things could have gone a lot differently. My positive outlook and my personality have been shaped by the great experiences of my life, my family, their love and the successes. Maybe I feel a little guilt for those who had similar challenges or were worse off and haven't done so well. I know I do have a sense that I owe those who couldn't manage. In fact, I would guess a lot of people had similar experiences without the loving environment I was fortunate to have had. I could see how that would be crushing.

Without that family closeness and support, I suppose those other things could have been too much to bear. I am sure that has been the case for many. Because of this I feel lucky, and I feel I owe it to the world to give back. I feel I need to leverage my skills, good intentions, experience and advantaged position in life and do something greater than I have so far.

There are many moments in life that shape a person's being. They form the basis for motivations that drive actions or behaviors in our lives. For many people, those experiences can actually be too painful or scary for them to deal with or discuss openly. These are the types of things that might keep many people who could really make a difference from coming forward. I understand this. It is hard—maybe impossible—for some to bare their souls to the world. The professional or personal risk of sharing their deepest vulnerabilities caused by their most personal experiences would be too much for them to take when they haven't even come to terms with them yet, themselves. There could be risk to their careers, to their family lives and to their positions in the community. Those reasonable fears keep people from openly supporting causes that might have been associated with some of their most challenging experiences.

While some might handle adversity well, others might experience very profound effects. I once knew a promising young man who took his own life due to the dark secrets of a past he must have hid from most people from early in his youth. There are others who have fought the demons that were brought forth by their experiences and are still struggling to this day. In my life, I would consider myself lucky in that I always had my family, love and support. I could handle any adversity that might have arisen. I feel there are so many people who can't handle their past and don't know how to express their feelings, and because of this, things just haven't turned out well for them. I feel compelled to do a lot, to cover a lot of ground, to lend support in a way that utilizes my strengths and skills. There are others who are better positioned to help, who are more in tune with the specific issues. Through my efforts and my work, hopefully I can help them to do even more.

Your deepest motivations for action could be dark secrets or innocuous life experiences. They could be the examples set by others or the obligation that you feel to give back as a result of your incredible success. Whatever inspires you to move forward, whatever stirs you to take up action, whatever it is that motivates you—you must harness this and understand it so that you are able to convey the personal nature of your connection to the cause, and your vulnerability, which allows others to share their motivations with you. Maybe it is time you dealt with those things from your past. Maybe digging deep is what will lead you to a personal breakthrough and provide the motivating force behind your move to philanthropy. The commonality of our experiences brings us together, and your influence is stronger when you lead those who are looking for support and guidance. Our icons know this; they have lived it. They learned there is power in identifying and reconciling with their experiences to turn them into motivations for their actions.

SELECT YOUR CAUSE
Or at Least the Organization

You can take your strongest motivations and strengths and get directly involved, running your own organization, or you can be involved while others tackle the issue. You need to understand that you don't necessarily have to run the show to drive the effort. Your influence can move others to act. It is about the effort and involvement you apply. This goes back to our earlier discussion about strengths. Identifying that your greatest strength is not to run the organization is as critical as taking the helm and leading a project. The outcome of your actions must be the impact. While commitment is necessary to lead philanthropy, there are different types of involvement, just as running various businesses requires various kinds of work. Great leaders would be nowhere with no one to lead. It takes the assembly of a quality team or support group, the delegation of duties, the identification and maximization of skills and the pressure of accountability to drive a project. Defining the roles in an organization and selecting those who can excel in these roles is the sign of a great leader. Look at your team today. What's working? What's not?

Now make a decision. Apply this approach to your social enterprise or look for those kinds of qualities in organizations you intend to support. Does this enterprise need you to run it, or will your guidance and expertise be better used to serve those who are more experienced and in touch with the cause? Can you apply your efforts as a mentor, donor, board member or adviser just as effectively as you could as a CEO, CFO or other executive? Would you make the best salesperson for the organization because of your motivation and immense passion for the cause?

As you review the possibilities, decide whether you will take control or have others lead while you advise. Your goal will be to inspire and lead a great organization to support your cause. By first identifying your role based on your motivations and strengths, you will be able to move forward in building this great organization.

There are so many more things that make up a great charitable organization. The bottom line is that they help improve the situation of the beneficiaries of the cause. There are many ways this is achieved and measured. The successful organizations exemplify this.

In my observations and research, I have come across what I think are the seven most telling qualities of a great organization. In no particular order of importance, they are:

- **Efficiency**—an organization must exhibit efficiency in the delivery of its support to the beneficiaries of its effort. It is about getting the most achievement for the least amount of effort—or dollars.

- **Transparency**—this is true of any organization or relationship. The least amount of organizational layers combined with full and true disclosure of all facets of the enterprise will attract donors and result in a greater connection with beneficiaries.

- **Access**—the openness of your executive team and directors to outside support and input will allow your organization to grow and instill confidence in all of your stakeholders.

- **Simplicity**—a simple hierarchy and a plain message will reduce the complexity of your cause to a simple problem with a perceivably simple solution. This will be a message that helps you to convey your mission to a broader audience and engage more support.

∞ **Financial Support or Need**—a clear definition of what your organization requires to successfully help its beneficiaries is critical. This defines how much funding or assistance you require and who gets what and to what benefit. It is not always the need that encourages the giving, but the clarity of the description of that need. Donors and benefactors know they want to help a particular cause, but the causes that most clearly articulate their needs and their desired outcomes will be looked upon first.

∞ **Fiduciary Prudence**—this quality addresses the fact that running a non-profit organization is truly a challenging financial task. The intricacies of managing donor funding for both sustainability and immediate use are complex. Organizations that can clearly communicate and fully understand their roles as fiduciaries will instill confidence in donors. Recognizing their place as stewards of beneficiary capital will allow a constant focus on the critical needs that must be met with the funds they have raised. This eye-on-the-prize approach means that decisions made with financial assets will always be consistent in keeping with the ongoing and future liabilities of the organization, not the egos or pride of the board or executives.

∞ **Governance**—this heavily discussed quality is a crucial factor in all organizations, for-profit included. The conduct of the executives and the organization as they act in the best interests of the beneficiaries and as a responsible corporate entity must be at the highest levels possible. Managing any enterprise responsibly is paramount to success and building trust with all stakeholders.

While the above mentioned seven qualities that define great organizations can be easily understood in theory, they are often overlooked by well-intentioned donors. In their efforts to give or help, donors might choose to look past the various shortcomings of an organization, rationalizing the gaps by suggesting that because the groups are charities they might not have all the necessary resources to deliver all seven qualities. The challenge with this is that as the lacking attributes begin to pile up, the donors' gifts or investments rapidly become diluted and the desired impact on the cause is lost.

I have highlighted a few of the types of organizations a donor must be aware of in order to avoid contributing to situations where they will not be achieving the most impact or the most direct effects possible. Below are five generically labeled types of organizations below, which encompass many variations of dysfunction.

- ✎ **The Inefficient Organization**—this organization wants to do well, really works hard and makes its stakeholders feel like they are having an impact. But it carries a lot of deadweight and utilizes its resources poorly. Its beneficiaries are shortchanged by inefficient financial management. This can be caused by unqualified people running the enterprise, too few people doing too many things poorly or, even worse, a massive force of people attacking a small challenge and expending far more resources than necessary.

- ✎ **The All-Sizzle, No-Substance Charity**—this organization is characterized by flashy fundraising campaigns or hot-topic causes, but in the end it is about the event and not about the cause. I was just shown a very glossy brochure and marketing package for a local non-profit entity. The package must have cost $100,000 to create. The pages were artfully done, but with maybe two or three words on each. The "ask" was unclear, and the funding options were limited and obscured by all the other packaging. So much more could have been said for so much less. Oftentimes after fundraising has occurred, funds do not get to the neediest organizations and end up in pet projects that might not have significant impact at all. There is an unhealthy belief in the premise that to make money you need to spend money. While this might be true in some cases, it is not always the case, and the reputational risk is sometimes far too great when it appears non-profits are spending wastefully while asking for financial support at precisely the same time.

Administration, marketing, promotional and operational costs in this organization are typically supported by the culture of the organization, but would be deemed as wasteful to outside viewers.

∞ **The Conflicted Charity**—at first this type of organization appears to have things together. Its financial situation seems sounds, and stakeholders appear to have a lot of skin in the game. This is something business types love to see. It shows that the risk and commitment level is significant, and thus the assumption is that the organization will exercise prudence in administering its efforts.

While it is never truly intended, a lot of these organizations find themselves in varying levels of conflict. Often this occurs when board members, who are significant donors, become heavily involved in an operational capacity directing the organization. Their intent is good, but the result is a complicated tangle of conflicts and future challenges for executives and next-generation board members. Self-dealing is another indicator of such conflict. This results when the charitable organization is more focused on the executive team's interests or agenda and less on the beneficiaries. Often disproportionate amounts of funds are spent on personal or employment-oriented initiatives designed more to sustain the business (to the benefit of salaried employees) than to sustain the cause.

∞ **The Ineffective Organization**—this organization often suffers from well-intentioned, under-qualified people with a goal to achieve great things but without experience, knowledge or the sophistication necessary to maneuver an organization through the fundraising and funding process — not to mention day-to-day operations. These people want success more than anything because they are deeply motivated, but they lack all the tools to get the job done. You will want to help them, but will soon understand that your efforts will be wasted.

↗ **The Outright Scam**—often this entity takes the form of tax reduction (read: avoidance) scams, investment schemes or even false front businesses. We have heard of this time and time and again; it makes for sad, but intriguing, headlines. The detrimental effect these operations have on all legitimate organizations is significant. Other entities may prey upon charitable organizations.

One of the most recent high-profile cases would be Bernard Madoff's Ponzi scheme. While never labeling his investment firm as a philanthropic organization, he willingly convinced heads of investment committees and non-profit organizations to invest their capital—all of it—in his scheme. While he carries the largest burden of responsibility, the organizations that invested their capital (often an inordinate amount of funds) with him had failed to uphold most of the previously mentioned seven important qualities of an organization. An organization that willingly invested all or most of its capital with Madoff clearly did not exercise transparency or fiduciary responsibility and did not have strong governance in its investment policies. If it had, the board of directors and donors might have had more input. If they hadn't been granted more input, then there would have been serious conflicts of interest that might have come into play in the decision to invest with Madoff.

Whatever your motivation or intention, whatever you decide—whether you will be starting your own organization or leveraging the strengths of an existing one—if you can amplify the best qualities and filter out the negative structures and practices, you will have already positioned yourself to have a greater impact.

Ultimately our goal in philanthropy is to help or support—to make a difference for the better. That outreach, if delivered honestly and effectively, will change the lives of many and could affect future generations. These are just a few of the simple and best practices and pitfalls that are present in many business settings today.

One of the greatest observations I have made about the "bad" organizations is that rarely, unless it comes through taxation (through the CRA or IRS), are these infractions and inefficiencies corrected. It might have something to do with the fact that in a philanthropic setting, a donor will give and expect no financial gain or direct tangible reward. In most cases it is believed that the beneficiaries of the funding or resources are too "frail" due to their needs, and that they are unwilling or unable to hold the organization accountable. I mean, really, how can a person bring themselves to sue an organization that, for example, feeds the homeless? By suing the executives or board, one could put the charity out of business, thus preventing meals from reaching those who need them the most. Does the saying "Don't bite the hand that feeds you" mean anything? Regardless, there seems to be a lack of accountability in the non-profit world. Charitable organizations would do well to have more consistent (and mandatory), higher standards of governance and regulation. The problems are largely systemic and tough to solve. A transparent method of ranking these organizations would do a lot of good in directing funds into the best and most reliable outcomes.

While there are few differences among great organizations in both the for-profit and not-for-profit worlds, there are enormous differences among the for-profit and not-for-profit organizations that are poorly managed, ineffectively run or just plain bad ventures. In the business sector, these kinds of enterprises are allowed to fail and be absorbed into the system. In the non-profit sector, these entities are carried along, in essence becoming charitable causes themselves. It would seem to go against the principle of giving to allow a charitable organization to fail, as though the beneficiaries were being let down. However, the reality is that these poorly run organizations are hampering the delivery of service and care to those who need it. They make donors more wary in their giving and less open to other, well-run organizations. Ultimately, they do much more harm than good. While it is the right thing to do to let these entities fail, it seems heartless on the surface. There is a great opportunity for business-minded leaders to help change this belief.

KNOW YOUR STRENGTHS
And Rely On Them

I have said that I believe that motivation leads to involvement and involvement leads to commitment, and philanthropy requires commitment. I would expect, by now, you have started to have a clear idea of the things that motivate you to want to give more, to do more. I am most certain that you have been able to connect your own personal experience with commitment to a task, to business building and corporate expansion. The things that inspire and move you to act and those forces or experiences that sit deep within you are what allow you to empathize with others. You may have a shared experience of one kind or another and you might only now be realizing that your circumstances are different. You are one of the fortunate ones. You have lived a charmed life, a rich life. You have worked hard and earned every cherished moment, but you must acknowledge the result of your lifelong dedications is that you are in very elite company.

I would also hope that at this point of the book, your interest in giving and openness to these ramblings have inspired you to consider just how you would do things differently—how you could combine your giving habits and your business skills to strive for only good outcomes and make every effort you put forth have an impact in this world. It is possible, and you have seen how others have committed and thrived.

I have just recalled something that I must bring up. It came from a story of the Maharishi Mahesh Yogi, told by Deepak Chopra in his Seven Spiritual Laws of Success about how the Maharishi wanted to organize a massive pilgrimage and attract hundreds of thousands of people to the event. However the Maharishi was very poor and there were little financial means to begin the effort. In his planning, the Maharishi was pressed by one of the organizers, who asked something along the lines of "Sir, this pilgrimage seems noble in its intention and significant in its size. How do you suggest we pay for all this? Where will the money come from?" The Maharishi replied, "It will come from where it is now." Talk about commitment! He was committed to his belief that if he put his goal of the pilgrimage out there in the universe and was sending a positive message with good intention, somehow that positive void would be filled and the funding for his efforts would materialize. And it did: the event was funded.

Now that might be commitment that is beyond even your aspirations, but it is not outside the realm of possibility to commit to a seemingly outlandish vision and make it happen. Your experiences have revealed that often those things that seem unachievable can be achieved. The impossible is possible.

So if you are prepared to move forward, let's go.

Let's address ways we can give. I'll highlight three of the top ways to give, and you can begin to think how your time, effort, money and resources fit in. I would say that money, time and influence are the broadest categories that would encompass giving. Those three things represent the sum of the myriad ways to give.

Giving Money

While it is clear that money is the obvious resource, you can also give products, goods, business services, etc. Any gift of a tangible asset represents money in this sense. This is something that most anyone who is reading this book has given. You've likely given some form of cash donation to some organization over time. There is the Halloween UNICEF box, the collection plate at church, the fundraising bake sale, the silent auction and even straight up donations of cash gifts, large and small, directly to a charity. Giving money seems simple and direct, and it meets what appears to be every non-profit's greatest need—more money. The trick is, it is easy. It is detached. And like most other monetary transactions, it is impersonal, not typically financially rewarding and usually consists of only what you can afford to give, so it doesn't "hurt" much.

Money could even be given—or rather, loaned—in micro-loan programs. Take, for example, Nobel Prize winner Muhammad Yunus, a Bangladeshi banker, who founded the Grameen Bank to specialize in giving loans to poor entrepreneurs. These micro-loan programs go where no typical bank or government program will go and provide much-needed capital to those who are looking for some small assistance in supporting themselves by starting or furthering a very small enterprise or business. This concept has caught on, and many of these programs exist worldwide. In fact, the age of social media has pushed the idea of giving into a variety of networks and made it extremely simple to give to the loan programs online, which in turn provide financing for various small businesses that fit the networks particular criteria.

Giving money is likely your strongest connection to charity thus far. In fact, it is also quite likely this form of giving was something you wanted to explore, which might be why you are reading this book. The impersonal financial gift has been your past experience. Well, we are looking to find involvement that is more meaningful. A move from impersonal giving to involved philanthropy is what we are seeking.

It would be quite simplistic to suggest that Bill and Melinda Gates along with their friend Warren Buffett have made extraordinarily large monetary gifts and that they rank highly in the financial giving department. I believe there is much more to the relationship between

Bill and Melinda and Warren Buffett and will explain the Gates' gift of influence in a short time. I would say that an early difference between the Gates' and Warren Buffet would be that Bill and Melinda Gates had involved philanthropy in their lives, while Buffett, at first, did not. His decision to give was financial—practical—for him.

Giving Time

Volunteerism is the broadest-reaching form of giving with the most direct impact. Volunteering can take many forms. As everyone knows, time is a precious commodity, which many of us feel is in scarce supply. You will be amazed at the massive impact just a little time can have. Cobbled together from wasted minutes throughout your days, weeks or years, time is not as scarce as you would think. In fact, the translation of time into a commodity can be viewed in volunteering as a high-reward endeavor. Finding the minutes and hours of your time to give is a priceless endeavor.

There are almost endless amounts of ways we can give our time. Give your time to directly—and manually—assist an organization. Next to money, and in some cases, ahead of money, man-hours are one of the most valuable commodities charities are often desperately lacking. You can do this by serving food to the hungry, building shelters for the homeless, providing much-needed professional services to an organization, cleaning your city, mentoring youth or providing advisory services to those who require the educational support. All are necessary and useful methods of volunteerism. Knowledge and expertise are valuable things, and charities, like all businesses, require strong guidance in their activities. You can build houses, be a Big Brother or Big Sister, coach sports, teach music or even just provide a listening ear or comforting shoulder. Time spent in this capacity will provide you with immediate and fulfilling rewards. There is a sense of accomplishment that you will immediately feel. You understand you have an impact that you can see and touch and feel inside.

In 2010, one of the largest quakes to hit the Caribbean in history struck Haiti. The island nation was shaken to its foundations. Many people rushed to Haiti's aid. Of all people, Bill Clinton appeared on the ground, lifting a shovel to help dig out the ruin. It was not merely a camera opportunity; it was willful action. This was a major act of volunteerism from a man who clearly might have been able to help in other ways. There was no sound bite required, no political agenda and no need for marketing. To give his time and volunteer in that situation was an extreme act of volunteerism. For all his presidential foibles, Bill Clinton has moved beyond merely being a figurehead for political attention or a fundraising focal point. He has truly grasped his purpose and the purpose of his philanthropic efforts and put them into action.

Giving Influence

I believe that giving influence has been the most consistent and unifying theme among every philanthropist, non-profit leader, volunteer, donor, etc. Giving your name, your leadership or your encouragement to an effort to convince, attract or engage and enlist more people to share your passion for the cause is an immeasurable way to give. For this reason, I personally believe this is the most important way a philanthropist can give.

When I posed the question, "What would you consider to be your most rewarding experience in philanthropy?," those I have interviewed unanimously cited their influence on others who became involved. While this is an oversimplification, as each person described vastly different specifics, the end result was the same. One philanthropist took great pride in having his friends open their considerably large cheque books and write similarly large cheques, while others were gratified to have turned many more eyes to their most important causes. The focus of attention on issues that would never otherwise garner a second—or even first—look was considered success by most everyone. Awareness was raised and efforts by peers were added, and in turn that moved others to act. The collective value of the influence and numerous eyes on a project helped shed light on the growing concern of success, while wallets were stretched to fund critical research. These were results of the giving of influence that were consistently noted. To give is noble, but to influence others to give is an art.

Just look at Oprah Winfrey. Her influence and reach is global. Her influence on tens of millions of Americans on a daily basis is palpable. When Oprah makes an impactful comment, gives a major gift or launches a new charitable initiative, the world knows immediately—and often follows suit. Look at the massive influence she had on North Americans to take up the Livestrong bracelet promotion when she had Lance Armstrong present his story and his initiative to help combat cancer on her show. Her book club not only inspired new interest in reading across North America, it also engaged millions in new discussions on literacy. When Oprah suggested a book for the club to read, the book's starving author highlighted on the program suddenly found that they would be financially comfortable for a long time. People started to read more, but they weren't just reading—they were talking about what they read. Neighborhood book clubs sprouted everywhere, and active, even formalized discussions on literature became part of the 21st century American culture. When it comes to influence, Oprah is a rock star.

Speaking of rock stars, Bob Geldof certainly understood the influence needed to move millions worldwide to open their hearts and wallets to give to combat the famine in Africa. One event after twenty years, his hit song "Do They Know It's Christmas?", still moves people to give and reflect during the holidays.

Now Bono has taken another approach. While basking in his various theatric personas, he has used the stage and his charisma to influence millions of people to think, engage and unify. However, it isn't the legendary rock personality or cult-like fan following he would likely suggest is his most influential trait. It is his audacious, in-your-face, one-on-one challenging of political figures in the bright lights of the public arena to do more, to be better and to keep their promises, that is most powerful. Bono's pressure on former Prime Minister of Canada Paul Martin started in 2003 and was reapplied in 2004. Paul Martin reacted by providing $70 million to the Global Fund to Fight AIDS, Tuberculosis and Malaria, then giving an additional $100 million for an AIDS-focused international initiative. Some would suggest that he succumbed to the pressure of the intense spotlight, but it appears the public challenge worked to kick-start action at the highest level of government. Bono has also challenged former U.S. treasury secretary Paul O'Neill to open the U.S. government's big wallet after a ten-day tour of Africa together in 2002. The ensuing efforts of the Bush administration saw billions of dollars head to fight poverty and AIDS in Africa. Bono's influence is becoming legendary.

Finally, I'll explain why I think the Gates-Buffett giving relationship has been so powerful. It is partly because of the sheer size of the wealth involved. Secondly it also provides us with clear insight into the gift of influence. I would suggest one of the greatest achievements that Bill Gates might reflect on, if you were to ask him about the rewards of his philanthropy, would be his influence on Warren Buffett to pledge $31 billion worth of Berkshire Hathaway shares to the Bill & Melinda Gates Foundation in 2006. At the time, Warren Buffett was not a philanthropist in any sense of the word, but he was and still is extraordinarily wealthy, and when he gives, the monetary impact is, to say the least, significant. This definitely qualified his charitable giving as important, but did not immediately commit him personally as an involved philanthropist. The initial commitment to the Gates' began a philanthropic process for Warren Buffett that has led to one of the most ambitious fundraising efforts ever. Bill and Melinda Gates managed to convince Warren Buffett to gradually become involved as a true philanthropist in every sense of the word. It was the Gates' dedication to their philanthropy that first influenced Warren Buffett to give, but it was the understanding of the power and impact that he had in return that set him on the road to philanthropy. This gift of influence might be one of the most important examples of peer pressure ever.

Craft
YOUR INSPIRED PROCESS

So, do you get it? Have you figured out what your motivation is? What strengths do you bring to the table? Do you think you have what it takes to become an icon? Can you change the world? Are you willing to start now? Oh yes, I know it is daunting, but you can do it. In fact, you've done it before, in your own business. You've started something from scratch or combined interests to form a major business engine with influence, market share and profits, satisfied shareholders, all of those important elements. I just have to show you how to apply that knowledge and experience to the world of philanthropy. This is an area where the return is social impact and the tangible effects might not be revealed for generations. Your stakeholders aren't looking for financial returns. Your missteps might actually cost lives, but your inaction could cost many more. The world of social enterprise is what you need to learn. I want to help you get this thing going. You're inspired: now let's get to business. This is a new direction for you, but it doesn't have to be a departure from what you know. In fact, I'm pleading with you to leverage your best skills and surround yourself with people who excel at the things you don't.

I'll walk you through this thoroughly in this chapter. In the next chapter, I'll give you the tools and the step-by-step instructions—let's call it philanthropy for dummies—to get your team built, formulate your ideas and push this forward. We'll build a solid foundation upon which to build your philanthropic masterpiece.

Here's your first step: use your personal experiences and motivations to determine the cause(s) you will support. Discover what has influenced you in your life or what things have shaped you—both good and bad. What is it about the environment around you that you think you could improve? Maybe visit a Third World country and learn what challenges the people face every day of their lives. Most importantly, you must understand why it is that a particular cause or opportunity has captured your attention. Ignite the passion within yourself to seek a solution, find a cure or assist an ongoing cause. Your efforts must have meaning, and for you to attain your best results they must be personal. You have found this in your business life. When you are engaged and passionate about a project, you excel at it, and you motivate others around you with that energy.

Next, turn this into a mandate. The goal could be as broad as "Cure cancer," "Feed the homeless" or "Rescue a child from poverty." Or you might have something a little more intangible, like "Preserve ecologically sensitive land for future generations to enjoy" or "Make the world a better place." The mandate establishes what the "ends" are. The "ends" will be the goal and the ideal that materializes from your motivation for change. The "means" will explain how you intend to go about achieving your mandate. For some, more generalized or grandiose mandates could be a series of smaller mandates woven into a single statement. "Preserving ecologically sensitive land for future generations to enjoy" will require the identification of what lands are sensitive—which might entail scientific studies, surveys, etc.—then an understanding of how best to preserve it. Then you will need to clarify what people will be enjoying the ecological conservation. All humankind? A specific community of users? How do you define "enjoy"—using the land or appreciating it?

Your mandate will drive all other actions. A mandate must be driven by a cause. This is why your organization will exist. Its purpose will be to provide a solution to a problem. It will be far easier to assemble an effective organization if you are clear about what you intend to do. Let's look at one mandate—we'll use the goal to "Cure cancer." Well, how do you cure cancer? It is a scourge of our lifetime. It affects everyone. There is no family that, through a lifetime, will avoid being touched by this disease in one way or another. It is relatively easy to attract funding and support for this cause. It is prevalent and at the forefront of many people's minds, not to mention that cancer is ruthless and scary. That said you and your organization want to cure the disease. You cure a disease by finding out how and why it works, when and why it occurs and what can kill it or prevent it from occurring. This effort requires science and scientists and laboratories. It requires technology, computers, databases and test subjects. It will involve a lot of failures along the way. There will be politics to manage. There will be a need for roles to support, to administrate, to procure, to communicate, etc. You will select the right people based on roles within your organization that are clearly defined and directly linked to achieving your mandate. Your mandate is what all actions of the organization will be measured against.

Next we will need to figure out what strengths you bring to the table. This is something you will need to be able to divine from within. There are others leading charitable causes who have been doing this for years. They have been in the trenches and understand the nuances of the diplomacy required to maneuver through private donors, tough social issues, public opinion and government programs to get what they can't bring themselves. What is it that you bring? If it is money, then so be it. Figure out how to bring your money and more to the project. If it is leadership, then apply what makes you a great leader to the development of the organization or to an already existing organization so that it can expand and grow. A good leader will deconstruct the organization and identify areas of need or opportunity. Roles will reveal themselves to you, the leader, and it will be your job to fill them by attracting the best people for the job.

If you bring awareness or celebrity to the project, you need to understand the social impact you already have. Is it your leadership that makes you so identifiable? Or is it your charisma and the things you say? It will be critical to know whether you are capable of leading or whether your skill is to assemble people around you who lead and direct while you "sell." It is always a shame when a company rewards its most fantastic salespeople with management roles, which is an ineffective use of resources often leading to poor results. They aren't wired that way. They do not lead and organize; they charm and convince, and they get to the heart of what motivates people and compel them to act. The best salesperson closes business and moves on. This doesn't often translate into good management. A great manager or leader must nurture and grow their charges. They must build trust, motivate and guide as well as delegate and direct. Know what you excel at and who you are. What is your specific strength? How can you leverage your knowledge, experience, position, influence and skills to have the biggest impact?

Seek advisers who specialize in philanthropy. You might be new to the world of philanthropy. You might understand business really well and you might have some great ideas, but understand there is a lot to be learned from those who have made giving and charity their life work. They, as any passionate business person would be, are deeply entrenched in what they do. They understand the subtleties of getting things done in the non-profit sector. They have skillfully maneuvered the political waters and maintain the balance between volunteerism and employment. They understand that the investment return for donors is mostly intangible and they know how to make the connection that compels a benefactor to give. So seek out these people and listen to them. Ask them what they see as the greatest challenges and needs in their organizations. Use their wisdom to leverage your talents. They lead by example in their field; understand how they do it and apply it to your philanthropy.

When selecting an organization to work with, look for the seven qualities (discussed in Chapter 6) that make an organization stand out. You don't have to start your own grassroots entity. A big challenge of charity is that there is no direct (or healthy) business competition. It is a sector where the beneficiaries (customers) aren't often selective about whom they receive assistance from. If they were, they might be scorned, as the adage, "beggars can't be choosers" is applied. How can the recipients of someone else's charitable efforts question the delivery of their support? What right do they have to question a volunteer or a donor who are giving of themselves to assist a complete stranger? On the other side of the equation, donors sometimes find it difficult to quantify their "return on invested capital" and thus will not necessarily be able to determine—at least for some time—the actual effectiveness of the organization they are supporting. When they made their donation, they never expected any tangible return, nor did they expect that their funds would go straight to the beneficiary without some form of administrative or organizational cost. So how do they measure their impact? Why would they even attempt to? The pressure of the two biggest factors in charity, beneficiaries and donor support and contribution to progress, might also sustain dysfunction.

I recently attended a meeting where a well-known and respected person, who had participated for decades in the charitable community and made a significant impact on those around her, embarked on a rather subdued rant against the common commentary that there is too much redundancy in the non-profit world. Her feeling was that there was no redundancy, that the 19,000 organizations that provided support in the province of Alberta were diverse and served a number of areas. I will concede this is true. The areas served were quite diverse and the services provided encompassed a tremendous cross section of all our lives, from health and nutrition to arts and culture, from education and sports to advocacy groups and environmental and social support organizations. But even if they were evenly split across one hundred different categories, there would still be 190 organizations per category. The broad spectrum of coverage does not address the issue of competition. It does not acknowledge the fact that for every segment of the support pie, of the hundreds of organizations that made up a large slice, most were not competing to be great at what they did, but were competing to survive. The argument was made that if any of the overlapping groups failed to remain in existence there would be a dangerous void. The implication was that somehow all well-intentioned people are the right people for the job and that any organization that exists to help has merit—even if it can't exist without receiving handouts—and that this void would not be filled and those relying on the services of the organization would quickly fall into dire straits. My feeling is that the void would quickly be filled by more willing and more skilled organizations.

This is what I see as one of the most important issues of the non-profit world at this time. There is a need to add a competitive spirit and sense of urgency to solve problems, not sustain them. I mean, really, where is there a bigger conflict of interest than when trying to solve a social problem when it means putting you and your organization out of work? The majority of people employed and volunteering in the non-profit sector are passionate and driven, but you have to consider that for those deeply entrenched and enjoying their employment, fulfilling their organization's mandate means intentionally removing their purpose for getting up each day. There is a subtle but powerful aspect to this.

It is most clearly reflected in civil service. Consider those who might work for a municipality. If they were to actually solve the community's challenges within their government, they would find themselves out of work. Sustaining the problems, but not solving them might keep them employed for their entire career. In fact, I'll go a step further. While we all want cures for diseases, imagine all those whose livelihoods would be negatively affected by success in this.

You can feel these undercurrents at this very time, in the multiple sclerosis research community. What if the Italian physician, Paolo Zamboni, actually has discovered a viable, repeatable and effective treatment? What if his assumptions are correct and all prior research has to be adjusted? It would mean that thousands of researchers hired by global pharmaceutical companies and non-profit organizations could be out of work; their entire lives' repertoire of scientific knowledge turned on its head and possibly discarded. It would be a great situation for the millions suffering worldwide, but what about all those people who rely on the disease to pay their bills? You could draw parallels to the oil business, but it is far less controversial to suggest collusion among big rich oil executives than among those who are trying to help solve a serious medical disease.

I know this is a highly controversial position, and I understand that many well-intentioned people will be greatly offended by this, but I implore you to look deeper into this. It is critical to identify areas where this might exist and then find solutions to help improve the situation. I'm merely playing the role of devil's advocate. I am certain that there is a need for charitable organizations to supply services more efficiently and direct their support to their stated beneficiaries, not to holding the creaking ship together in every storm that brews. This would also ensure that the strongest and most efficiently run organizations would take the lead, take over other struggling entities and attract the most capital from donors while applying the best methods to help beneficiaries. The consolidation of many groups serving the same issue could be a powerful thing. Bringing together the best people with the greatest passion and applying a superior organizational and mandate-focused leadership structure could allow these great people to maximize their skills and deliver the highest quality service possible. There are incredible organizations that get it done right and could be modeled or joined.

If only beneficiaries could vote by choosing the best provider. We could get reliable market feedback on all of this. You have to realize this is a tough sell. If you were starving and the group on the corner offers you a meal, would you travel across town to the better-run group? Nope; you'd eat. If you were in a restaurant and you were paying for the meal, you might go to the better establishment. How about asking the beneficiaries for their opinion? Shareholders and customers of a normal business can vote with their money and their stock. If a company delivers poor service, it sells fewer items and its shares become less attractive, declining in real or perceived value. Such feedback is most often not available for non-profit groups, as their beneficiaries typically can be desperate for any help and their donors expect no financial return.

Now we need a plan. If organizations are allowed to fail and market forces provide valuable feedback on which businesses are succeeding and which are failing, then the successfully run groups must be there to pick up the pieces or fill in the emerging gap. Beneficiaries falling through the cracks of the system must not be the result. For example, let's say an organization is in place to both feed and shelter the homeless in a city. While another strictly delivers food to the homeless, there is yet another group providing warm beds to sleep in and not much else.

The shelter that provides food as well finds itself in a financial bind due to the poor management of its food services. Its staff members have lacked judgment and applied poor budgetary management to their kitchen. These circumstances threaten to close their operations down. They acknowledge that it is the food service portion of the business that they have mismanaged. It is the most costly, and it has put stress on their resources. For them to cease providing food would have a direct impact on their beneficiaries. They feel that men and women who rely on them would immediately be forced to go without much-needed meals. In good conscience, they cannot move to discontinue either offering. Thus they make the decision to limp along, with other services being affected, and eventually this dysfunctional situation will lead to their demise. They rationalize their situation by suggesting that provision of some service is better than none.

The other organizations that specialize in only one of the two services are thriving. The food service group is comprised of specialists in procuring food, and they excel at the preparation and delivery of their services. The room-only group has been in the business of providing shelter for decades, and has no unusual space costs or infrastructure needs. These two groups are working from a position of financial and operational strength.

All three are working parallel to each other in a sense, but are also reliant on each other in some way. If one goes out of business, all three might be affected as those receiving help from the suffering organization will soon seek out help from the others. This could overwhelm them. By providing emergency funding and sustaining the poor business model of the entity that provides food and shelter, systemic pressure on all agencies can be avoided, or at least delayed. But sustaining the operations of a group that cannot run its operations economically or be prepared to change will perpetuate bad practices that will lead to the inevitable deterioration of a much-needed service.

To allow the organization to fail might be a short-term nightmare, but with enough prior knowledge, the two single-focus organizations might be able to mobilize to prepare for such a possibility and form some logical working relationship. Another possibility is that one of the two or a strategic combination of both could completely take over the operations of the dual-purpose entity. This might in fact be the best solution. There is so much pushback and such tunnel vision in some non-profit organizations that they are hesitant to seek help or admit failure when their operations are at risk, or they will leverage their predicament for a fundraising campaign. That is not the answer to sustainability, nor is it an answer to the challenges faced by their beneficiaries.

Sometimes poorly run for-profit businesses fail. And they are allowed to fail. In fact, their competitors have already planned for what they would do in such a case. That is what should be encouraged to naturally occur in the non-profit sector as well. There must be growth in the sector to support this. That is, the organizations providing the same or similar services must be aware that the possibility exists that those entities that fall on hard times (due to internal problems) might not be bailed out and instead will be allowed to fail. In this case, these other providers will make preparations to fill the gap. This type of thinking would allow for continued growth and improvement. Without this market force, too many poorly managed organizations continue to survive. Their fundraising efforts become an act of self-provision instead of providing for beneficiaries. Keeping a business in business isn't always the same as providing for those it serves.

Where do the opportunities lie for you to help? While I have spent some ink on describing a rather tough-love view of the state of some organizations in the non-profit business community, I would suggest there is a great upside to all of this. Those of you who have the skills, developed and refined in your business experiences, might be able to provide some of the solutions. One such solution would be in the area of mergers and acquisitions. Many great businesses evolve from the sequential accumulation of businesses by a single entity. In the non-profit sector, the possibility exists that one organization might have a great vision to aggregate other businesses in an effort to best serve a specific social need, and leaders with experience in mergers and acquisitions can realize this. A well-run charity with a good eye for the bottom line as well as a strong social return can serve as a template that other organizations can base themselves on. Recognizing the opportunities that consolidation or, at the very least, collaboration offer will lead to stronger growth, innovative thinking and a greater chance of sustainability.

If you have led a business through this and can apply that expertise with the sensitivity required to understand all aspects, then you can offer a genuinely progressive viewpoint. As I mentioned earlier, this is not your traditional domain, and non-profit organizations have unique challenges and politics. It would behoove any new participant coming from a business background to listen to the experiences of the leadership group in the charitable setting and work to gain a better understanding of these things.

When it comes down to it, there are plenty of opportunities to apply yourself in the non-profit sector, but you must understand that the system is not broken, just different. Where needed improvements can be made there will be great support from the people. The fundamentally important key to all of this is to constantly be aware that giving is about the beneficiaries. These organizations exist to help or do good. If you act in a manner that is consistent with the mandate of the organization from the outset, you will find acceptance and cooperation.

This is how you would do it in your business. Do it in your philanthropy.

Execute

YOUR INSPIRED PROCESS

Okay, there has been a lot of talk from me. There have been a lot of examples of others who have done great things. Let's see if we can get you started on the road to philanthropic greatness. I will admit this was a chapter of my book that I really put off writing. I found it rather mundane and methodical instead of thoughtful and insightful. But I suppose this is something that needs to be embraced, as well. It needs to be truly understood. The strategic art of the execution of philanthropy can be inspiring. The 30,000-foot view is a must for you. The specifics are critical for your team. I understand that you have not spent your time building intricate systems or supporting complex tasks, but you have most definitely driven them. You have inspired and initiated them. Your goal was to assemble the team that would bring your visions to reality. To execute your plans, you needed an understanding of the process. In order to understand the challenges faced by your team, you needed to know what it would have to do to get things accomplished. In fact, the more you knew about the process, the more you could also troubleshoot with or question your team. Your knowledge has always been applied through your vision.

The first step, now that you know your motivation, your cause and the strengths you bring to the table, will be to set up your support system. As in any business, you will need to do some market research. Understand your competitors and know the market you will be serving. Also decide if you will be creating an entity or if you will be supporting an existing one. Your market review will very likely lead you in this decision. You will either be inspired by an organization that can use your expertise and is aligned with your personal and philosophical views or you will believe that your unique vision is better suited to an start-up organization. Either way, your research will help you make your decision.

Establishing an endowment, foundation or trust to direct your funding through will still be a good starting point. There are many professionals in the legal and accounting world that can direct you and establish the formal entity for you. You can find these people by investigating online, asking your trusted advisers or inquiring with your established community foundations.

The establishment of a foundation provided Bill and Melinda Gates with a "holding tank" for the capital they were able to invest as well as raise from others. Many entities (charities and businesses) have been spawned by these organizations. The same was the case for Bill Clinton. His lucrative speaking engagements garnered him a substantial living post-presidency, but there were both tax incentives as well as charitable motivations that led him to forming a foundation. The knowledge that proceeds from an event will be directed to a charitable foundation often makes the significant cost of a meal or a table much more palatable for participants. There is also a clear understanding that some of the funds will be used to support Bill Clinton in his travel, accommodations, etc. for the engagements. No one believes or expects that his philanthropy comes without some sort of cost. The foundation can be the storing facility for the capital that will, in time, be redirected.

The benefits of having an entity established, even without setting up a specific organization, are that you will have somewhere to move or direct funds as you gain support. The initial establishment of such a structure might have tax implications; you should discuss these carefully and thoroughly with your accountant and/or an accountant who specializes in tax advice for charitable transactions.

Earlier I highlighted a comment from Sergey Brin. He suggested that he preferred establishing a business that pursues philanthropy and charitable ends rather than forming an actual charity—that forming a business with charitable goals sets the tone for an approach that is innovative, profit-oriented and structured accordingly. The existence of a formal infrastructure helps define roles and determines the most efficient use of capital while aligning financial efforts with the mandate of the organization.

Following are some basics that you need to know when creating your own charitable organization:

- Consult with the appropriate professionals. Seek out qualified accountants, tax advisers and lawyers who specialize in the establishment of advisory services for charitable trusts, foundations, endowments, etc. They will help navigate the formation of such entities, steer the tax-efficient movement of capital to them and provide guidelines for the receipt and movement of capital to and from them.

- Next, construct your business plan by starting with the vision, mandate and mission statement. You have done this numerous times before. This is basic business planning 101. Your organization will be a business in every aspect, except for the way it moves its capital. The nuances of capital flows and donor-beneficiary relationships are unique to the non-profit sector, but for the most part the end requirements are the same as in the for-profit sector. Communicate your plans and achievements effectively and transparently. Report on how you intend to monitor progress and summarize success and growth over time. Providing constant feedback tailored to your stakeholder groups is paramount.

- As you establish your presence, it will be important to identify those people and organizations who will provide assistance, those who will be suppliers and those who you will support and make efforts to integrate with through a common goal. When these synergistic groups understand their role and their position in the process of setting up your organization, they will be more effective at supporting your initiatives. Those who work with and support the philanthropic community understand that it takes a village to raise a child, and put this into practice more often than most for-profit businesses. This shared community vision of doing good is unique. Those supporting cast members will range from accountants, lawyers and financial advisers to office suppliers, marketing professionals and landlords.

∽ Other important areas to focus on include governance and board establishment. While it is not mandatory to quickly establish a board of directors, it is a good idea. The governance issues are very similar to those in any business approach. Governance will be improved through consultation, understanding principles and best practices, establishing policies and procedures, creating manuals and keeping everything documented. There are exceptional organizations that provide specific consultation on governance and best practices for charities. Look for those niche organizations and review their past and current clientele to get an idea of their experience and strengths.

Establishing good governance guidelines is an important step, but a more important step is to follow those best practices while incorporating good governance into your organization's daily activities. As you know from your business experience, the individuals responsible for carrying this out would be those comprising the board of directors.

As in any business, the board of directors is established to be a voice for the stakeholders. The directors are there to provide guidance and evaluation for the executives of the organization. Their direction falls mainly to the hiring and guiding of their primary employee, the chief executive officer (CEO). The board serves as the owner-representative and as the servant-leader. "Carver's Policy Governance® Model in Nonprofit Organizations," by John Carver and Miriam Carver (2001), is a great article that explores the governance model and its application in the non-profit sector. The voice of the stakeholders of the enterprise is reflected by policy set and observed by the board of directors. Stakeholders can be members of a group or the community as a whole. Moreover, there is a clear moral equivalent to "ownership." The board is the on-site voice of those owners. Additionally, the board must take the role of servant to the owners before its leadership role in the organization. It must lead the organization subject to its discoveries about judgments of the values of the ownership.

A board does not direct executives or staff on how to conduct themselves. It does not create policy, build business plans or implement strategies. It is there to review the plans, make recommendations and suggestions to improve them and to review the governance issues faced as a result of decisions made. It is definitely part of the advocacy group and might be able to make important introductions for executives, as well as provide referrals to experienced professionals or people who might be able to assist an organization, but it is not expected to be involved daily in the regular activities of the organization. It communicates its directions through the CEO it has hired to run the organization. The CEO is directed under its authority. The board will provide the autonomy necessary to allow this person to do their job effectively.

Next you will need to assemble the team to run this organization, something you have done time and time again. We are not going to suggest there is anything particularly unusual here. One professional you might seek to fill a particular role not typically found in the for-profit world is the director of fundraising. This person will be well-versed in how to make the "ask" for funds. They will clearly understand how to approach donors or donor groups. They will have a working knowledge of and be able to contact people who can support sophisticated giving and planned giving projects. You establish the requirements of the organization, and then the roles for fulfilling the goals and carrying out responsibilities are defined. The right people who are most suited for the roles are then uncovered and put into place. A common mistake is developing a role around an individual or a group of individuals. Clearly defining the roles of your organization without the employees in place will allow you to construct the best plan possible. Then, identifying and inserting the best-suited people will be highly effective.

Here is a list of the key roles in your organization:

- CEO/executive director/president/general manager
- CFO/treasurer/controller
- VP fundraising and donor engagement
- VP operations
- Beneficiary liaison/advocate
- VP marketing and communications

After the above steps are completed, you have essentially established the framework for your organization. Next it is time to get to work.

As in any business plan, there are financial considerations. Balancing the funding of future and ongoing liabilities with today's assets and expected future cash flows is essential. You must construct a basic financial model that incorporates donations and investment returns as they affect revenue, expense and cash flows. As well, you must strive to develop a model that finds a large portion of all revenue going directly to the beneficiaries of your cause. It should be an innovative leader's goal to somehow quantify this or develop this as a form of reinvestment of earnings, where in some cases the funding of beneficiaries has some kind of return. This might be in the form of goodwill or even in capital return, but the ability to quantify the impact of your funding and demonstrate the accretive value of your efforts will greatly enhance your financial picture. Being able to convey your organization's impact in more tangible terms to your donor base can improve the engagement and advocacy of those donors as well as provide your organization with measurable milestones demonstrating your effectiveness.

While building your business plan, you must identify the costs of running the enterprise, differentiating the hard costs of being in business from the costs of funding your beneficiaries. There is a common misconception out there that charitable organizations are very inefficient with their capital. I would suggest there is a good case for the argument as it pertains to the management and deployment of financial capital. Developing new revenue sources and expanding sustainability are areas where this applies, but charitable organizations are highly effective at blending financial capital with human capital—in many cases, more so than for-profit businesses. The available resources in the volunteer sector at the disposal of non-profit organizations can be extensive. Quantified, this often means a greater efficiency in the entity's application of services or operations.

Where the misconception might lie is in the definition of efficiency versus profitability. Productive and efficient businesses create the most profit with the least amount of energy (money, human resources, productivity, etc.) expended. Profit is simple to measure in business—conceive goods, make goods, sell goods, collect revenue and measure profit; repeat. Profit is the end goal, not an intermediate step. The financial relationship in a large number of non-profit organizations ends quite some time before a measure of "profitability" can be realized. For example, if your goal is to create better environments for young people to learn in, and one of your deliverables is to feed those children, then your "profit" lies in the mandate—which is to enable them to learn better. So, over a childhood, this would be measured by the outcomes of test scores and academic achievements, not by the food they ate. The feeding step is very tangible and quantifiable. The improved learning skills are not so simply measured, but the "profit" lies in those future numbers. In fact, it could be argued that the "profit" is in the increase in future employers that would emerge from the pool of youth who were being fed better so that they could focus more on their academics, versus their growling tummies. This is the perpetual conundrum of measuring success—"profit"—for non-profit organizations.

Now we have our vision, our mandate, goals, roles, people, governance and financial parameters in place. The next stage is to consider reporting. Each role is filled by a person (or people) who will be required to report to another party about how their responsibilities are being executed. An organization must compile this information and package it to present to its board and to all its stakeholders. There will be marketing pieces, financial disclosures, board presentations, investment reports, beneficiary impact statements. Most of the reporting will be very similar to the reporting done in for-profit business. In fact, some of the necessary disclosure of the business sector would be a marked improvement to the disclosure and reporting in the non-profit world. In Canada, the CRA is the regulating authority. In the U.S. it is the IRS, state laws pertaining mostly to running corporations, the First Amendment and any applicable religious or human rights statutes. The reality of this is that regulations really account for the financial and tax reporting rules of the organization; outside of this, there is no other self-regulatory body that guides or creates policy that non-profit groups must adhere to. This leads to a significant lack of transparency in reporting. There are plenty of standards available out there. In fact, there are very well-defined best practices, governance and investment policies that have been carefully crafted as tools of the trade, but there is no self-regulatory body that is holding non-profit organizations to these standards.

The Meaning of
PHILANTHROPY
And Your Role

To become a great philanthropist, give with great purpose

Definition of Philanthropy

There are multiple definitions of philanthropy that seem, often, to conform to the point of view of the author. Quite a few explanations or definitions centre on improving or increasing the well-being of humankind through charitable donations or aid. The one that sticks, for me, is simple in its meaning: philanthropy is the practice of charitable giving; the word's Greek origin means "love of mankind." [11] I would suggest that this means that the focus or emphasis in giving is on the actual practice of doing so. This implies a concerted effort or habit of giving. To "love" mankind, to just sit there loving while doing nothing, does not seem to me to be philanthropic. There might be those who actually believe that if they think about a good cause long enough and support it through their beliefs, somehow they have actually helped it. But just because they wish it so, doesn't make it so. Directing funds here and there with benevolence seems closer, but still does not seem to me to capture the spirit of the practice of giving. The empathy involved and the altruism implied in giving are what begin to shape philanthropy. Next, the emotional and physical connection to the actual giving links the act with philanthropy. Where there is practice there is purpose. To engage with purpose allows a person to devote their strengths and passion toward a goal. Again, this embodies the commitment required to truly be philanthropic.

This is what separates the icons from the leaders; it is not a holier-than-thou approach where the philanthropist is never wrong or their acts never result in unintended consequences. The fallibility of individuals highlights that vulnerability, which allows them to engage, to understand and to initiate change. This, in turn, draws others in and attracts support. This influence, which comes from leading a cause with intention and vulnerability, augments a person's ability to drive a project forward.

In order to understand what it means to be philanthropic or have a charitable impact, it is also necessary to understand the beneficiaries of the act. It is critical to know what difference is being made and what difference matters most. This won't be known unless you've been a beneficiary, know one or have made the effort to understand them. Philanthropy is a human endeavor, and even if it is sometimes hard to match the beneficiary, it is important to know whether the beneficiary is your neighbor, your relative, your mother, or the family living in a mud hut thousands of miles away.

Admittedly, it is hard for those of us who have not been on the receiving end of charity, or those of us who have not felt particularly oppressed or wronged, to understand where our place in the global community is to help. Oftentimes, our thoughts focus on our own local community and the challenges faced by our immediate neighbors who might be less fortunate, stricken with illness or affected by disaster. This is good. This is our community conscience. Your help begins here.

But there is a bigger picture, and you need to understand your role in that picture. You need to understand the responsibility, locally and globally, that comes with the prosperity you and your family have enjoyed in life. No one is suggesting that by not giving you are any less deserving or that you are any less decent. You are not begrudged your prosperity for it. In fact, you are celebrated for all that you have accomplished. Your success in life is something to be cherished and protected. However, consider that with such blessedness comes responsibility. You are responsible to humankind to lead. This leadership can be shared with and mentored in others. The influence you have can move people to act. Your knowledge can stimulate innovation, and your money can give options to those who were born into a world where their options are dictated to them, taken away from them or limited to food, shelter and survival.

So, you start at home, and then you work your way into your community and the city in which you live. Soon you are giving to state or provincial organizations and feeling a connectedness to your country. But beyond that, what impact can you have? Why would you even bother going beyond your country's borders?

Make a Difference

If it is a problem in the African savanna, why is it an issue for us? Well, the fact is that turning our backs on millions of starving people while we enjoy bountiful amounts of food and nutrition disconnects us from the world. It moves us farther away from the understanding of our own prosperity. Politically, such events put our very lives and personal safety at risk. The unethical, immoral and power-hungry people who would take the opportunity of a drought to further their own causes by controlling the monetary and food supply while subjecting the population to obedience in the sake of power, harbor those who are interested in the same and will pay for their safety. Conditions of this nature provide the breeding ground for these unsavory maggots. The result of these breeding grounds is still clearly embedded in our memories of the Yemen bombings, Somalian uprisings and the 9/11 terrorist attacks—and, in turn, the retaliation that was carried out to seek and punish those who continued to pose a threat and oppress many world nations over the past ten years. The struggles of Africa's people and nations affect all of us. Their plight matters.

With over six billion people on this planet connected through technology, telecommunication, transportation and geography, the ripples in our human oceans can become tsunamis of unimaginable destructive force. It is in our best interests to make small, seemingly insignificant matters our problems, our causes.

Share Your Philanthropy

I know what you're thinking: boy that was moving! Yes, it was, and I would guess that you are now overwhelmed a bit, and think that those are issues that require much bigger solutions, much more funding and much more time and effort than you could ever offer. Well, you're right. They are.

I mentioned earlier in this book that there was one unifying theme throughout what all philanthropists, community leaders, charity executives and volunteers cited was their single most rewarding experience in philanthropy. That experience was influencing others. It was the ability of those people to leverage their skills, money, political position or knowledge to move and influence others to take up action for the cause. Not only is there strength in numbers, but there is enormous gratification in knowing that you were able to move others to act. The sense of community and belonging we feel when others share our vision or take up our cause or fight our fight is empowering. It emboldens us to persevere.

So, how do you do it? Well, start by leveraging those around you. Encourage their participation. Challenge them to imitate or match your behavior. How do leaders like you do it? You lead. You set unmistakable examples of behavior and dedication to a cause. Leverage your peers; they're probably as prosperous as you. Challenge them through your actions, or even challenge them directly.

ACCOMPLISHMENT
Is Nothing Without Reflection

I want to speak about something that is a very hard thing for a lot of entrepreneurs to do. The innovating, forward-moving personality traits of these high-achieving, driven people—you know who you are—tend to distract them from taking an inventory of the things that they have achieved or accomplished. Spending a few moments to focus on the positive achievements that have been accomplished is a must. This important aspect of achievement is critical to long-term happiness.

Imagine if you are unable to enjoy what you have accomplished because you are already looking ahead to the next horizon. Then imagine if you could never achieve true happiness. You will never find satisfaction in your life if your past wasn't good enough and your future isn't happening fast enough. This focusing on accomplishment is something that might be easier in for-profit business. The close link between the ego and the vision a business has will tend to give rise to a moment or two of excitement when they believe they have achieved something substantial. There will be celebration of the feat and some form of acknowledgement, just before the next day arrives and a new challenge is presented. This outward enjoyment of achievement is healthy, rewarding and can be used to bring more energy to the next great step. Once people begin to view their accomplishments as achievements that were earned, they begin to promote the concept of gratitude from within. Be grateful for having the good fortune to have been able to participate in something bigger than yourself and it will allow you the humility to place others' interests ahead of your own.

With a philanthropic endeavor, the characteristic of being unfulfilled by one's achievements can be exaggerated. In a lot of cases there is always much work to be done. Just think what a rare occasion it is when a charitable cause has been cured, retired, accomplished fully or rendered obsolete. There is little room for self-appreciation when the issues that others are facing are so much more challenging than yours. This alone can be enough to keep the hungry philanthropist from reflecting on any of their success. Now take it a step further and ask someone who has a philanthropic heart and a pure motive to help to revel in their charitable accomplishments and you'll be hard-pressed to witness them indulge in such behavior. When and if they do, it is typically in an apologetic and almost self-deprecating way. That said, frequently the cause is a serious matter and the best outcomes might be tiny dents in a massive wall, but successes must be enjoyed in order to derive more energy to tackle the next task. The philanthropist must find fulfillment and must be able to share it in order to remain focused and helpful. Naturally, I would not be suggesting a party with champagne and streamers for those who have just saved 1,000 people from starving when 500 more couldn't be saved, but I am suggesting the positive impact needs to be acknowledged and celebrated in its own appropriate way.

What is it that you are most proud of so far in your life of giving? Have you celebrated it? Take this moment now and recall the most recent significant philanthropic thing you have done and what your impact was. Do you understand how important your involvement was? Do you feel personal pleasure in the fact that you have been able to somehow enhance the lives of others?

When asked what they were most proud of, the overwhelming majority of philanthropists suggested it was the influence they had on others to act and help a cause, either by way of financial pressure or by their efforts to become personally involved, which in turn influenced others. It is interesting to observe that reflection on achievement comes as a product of creating a collective effort. To attract others to your own agenda and have them raise awareness, provide funding or solve a problem is personally gratifying, and is the indirect way a philanthropist can celebrate their impact. This safely removes them from the perception (either by others or even themselves) that they are receiving accolades for the good they do or from being self-impressed by their efforts. I think this is a step beyond simple humility. If the sole gratification that came from lending a hand was attracting others to lend a hand, then why wouldn't these philanthropists just start a membership organization called *Those Who Would Like to Help People Help Others?* I do believe these people are genuinely unconcerned about the honorable mention, so they really do gain a sense of accomplishment in their ability to draw others to their cause, but I also know there is more—in all of us. I think it matters to everyone that they actually helped solve a problem, save a person or better someone else's life. This is good. This is a great quality of humanity. There is an innate need to share life's experiences with one another and a fundamental need to be needed. To recognize this and celebrate it is a good thing.

Without this reflection, how will you know whether you made a difference? Measurement is the best way to determine if you have been effective. It will uncover opportunities to improve. Assessing the results will provide clarity and insight into the things that you have done well. You will be able to focus on the good things and provide further support to those efforts.

This reflection will tell you a lot about your experience in giving. It will tell you a lot about the effectiveness of your efforts. It will also reinforce why you are actually involved. Earlier in this book we discussed your motivations for giving to help you determine a cause that you could support that has deep personal meaning to you. The benefits you receive should somehow relate to your motivations. If you were once abused and that is the focus of your efforts, then helping a victim, enforcing the law or educating potentially high-risk offenders should provide you great satisfaction. If your efforts have not produced the results you hoped they would, then you will need to change your methods or reapply your efforts.

If you are a survivor of cancer or have been impacted by the disease, and if a cure has not been found but you are able to provide informed and emotional support to a person or a friend who is struggling in their fight with it, then there are small but very important personal achievements that you must reflect on. These things will help motivate you to continue your philanthropy. I have made a friend this year named Michael— at least I consider him a friend, although we have only met on a few occasions and have shared some personal experiences in conversation and through email. He is a cancer survivor, father, husband and an MBA grad. He tangled with cancer over fifteen years ago as a brain tumor tried to rewrite his life story for him. He had other plans, and he battled hard against the disease and the stress that it placed on his young family while enduring treatment. What Michael has shared with me has been very helpful as I try to understand gratitude and the importance of reflection on the good in my own philanthropy, as I perfectly fit the entrepreneur profile I described before—never satisfied with where I've been and impatient to get to where I'm going.

My first meeting with Michael was an interview for this book back in January of 2010. A friend said we should meet, as Michael had survived cancer and was on the board of directors for a chapter of the Canadian Cancer Society, so we did. Some of the key questions I asked people in my interviews for this book after finding out more about them personally were about their greatest achievements and challenges in philanthropy. I would end each session with a question that was intended to come across as a bit of a challenge: I would ask each person what they could do better. When confronted with this, Michael had a couple things to say. The first came from his experience with his own mortality. He made a commitment to himself to make a difference, to have an impact in the things he does while not holding his tongue when he felt his opinion would matter—he'd generally become a voice of reason or discontent opposing status quo thinking.

Next came a story of another cancer patient. The man's name was Ryan. Ryan was a young man, a successful financial adviser, a great husband and caring father to his young son and a very well-liked person in the community. Ryan had been diagnosed with terminal brain cancer that had begun to take his life from him, and it was doing an effective job, although never denting his tremendous spirit or great attitude about life. Michael used the story of Ryan to illustrate his own pledge to do better. And it came in the most intimate form. He would work harder to make an impact directly on those who had become confronted with the same diagnosis. He would make himself more available to those who were struggling with the news, with the next steps and with how their families were coping. This proximity to deeply personal experiences in such a giving way would bring Michael closer to the lives of people who, in a lot of cases, would not make it. I believe this is extremely courageous. The support that he can provide to those who are in desperate circumstances is immeasurable. The risk it places him in is significant as it draws him personally into the immense sadness of loss. The reward is that he can bring comfort and calmness to others in a chaotic situation. Michael would be there for Ryan and others like him.

Upon Michael's urging, I began to follow Ryan's blog and became engrossed in his daily struggle for normalcy in a dire situation. I became a part of the struggle, and I didn't even know the man personally. But along the way, I stopped reading. I had become busy at work, at home and with a number of things steering my attention away, until a day in June brought my focus back. It was that day a client of mine called to tell me her husband had been diagnosed, earlier in April, with terminal cancer of the brain and abdomen. He had been given three months to live. While we discussed things, we shared a lot; I listened a lot and offered the best help I could. I also told my client that I loved her and her husband, that I cared for them and that they could call upon me for pretty much anything they might need during that time. That was a first for me. I owed it to Michael. He demonstrated to me the need to allow myself to share my feelings openly, to be vulnerable and to offer my support in any way I could. After that call, I quickly checked back in to Ryan's blog. The site had a different tone to it. There hadn't been many entries lately. Ryan had died two months prior, in April on Easter Sunday. I sat in my office and cried quietly to myself. My client's husband passed on this July, and I shared the celebration of his life with his wife, his family and friends who loved him very much.

I have reflected on my effort to comfort and listen when people need me. I feel I shared an important and crucial part of life with people I care for—more deeply than is typical in my profession. In this reflection, there was a feeling of connectedness, of helpfulness. There was also learning. The experience reminded me to be more vulnerable, to share my true feelings with the people that are in my life and to become more intimate in my relationships with my clients and friends. For this I am grateful.

So, when you give, it is necessary to reflect on what you've accomplished. If you are really going to explore your philanthropy in every way, you will need the feedback regularly. The larger the issues you decide to tackle, the more challenges and possible failures will come your way. You will need to understand where your gratitude comes from; even through the smallest of accomplishments. This recognition will give you the strength to continue and move forward.

The
ONEFORONE MILLION
Challenge

At the outset of this project, I had every intention of creating a compilation of reading material that could provide readers with a unique look into what inspired some global icons to make the decision to devote their lives to philanthropy. I would use my experiences and numerous interviews of community philanthropists, charity workers, volunteers and business leaders to bolster my commentary. My initial idea was that it would be interesting to understand those icons better. Then as the project moved forward I realized the best outcome of my efforts and observations would be to have some leader in a position of wealth and influence read my commentary and find themselves moved to act. That would be my single-handed effort to shed some light on a particular subject, and it might be enough to influence and inspire another person to act.

My professional investment advisory practice has a similar goal. I constantly strive to apply my expertise as an investment adviser to leverage my skills and influence to improve the overall investment experience of non-profit organizations by at least one percent every year. That is one percent in cost savings, efficiencies, returns, and donor engagement, or whatever we can find to get there. And, my goal is to generate an additional $1 million dollars for every $100 million I am able to direct or advise and that can go toward a cause such as feeding people in need, sheltering families, or curing disease. I feel that is a phenomenal impact, and that is a goal I aspire to every day in my practice. I call that my OneForOne Million goal—one person improving many lives by adding one million dollars to the effort. I have identified my desire to help coupled with the motivation to do great things for organizations, with an end goal of having an impact of millions.

After working my way through to the end of this writing project, I have found that I have created the opportunity I had hoped for—that by reading this book, one person could be inspired to strive to affect one million "anything," whether through helping people, raising dollars, saving acres, making lunches, building homes, etc., by leveraging their skills, their motivations and their influence on others. To formalize this initiative, I have decided to launch the OneForOne Million Challenge. It is directed at you, my readers.

Just think: there was one of you—let's call him Bob Smith, CEO of SuperDuper Corp.—and these musings inspired him. Reading about Oprah got him going; in fact, last year his chemical company made more than Oprah is worth. What was she so capable of that he wasn't? With a plan, it didn't seem so daunting. Now inspired, Bob decided to kick things off by establishing the SuperDuper Foundation to cure diabetes. After all, Bob's physician just diagnosed him as a "borderline" diabetic. This sent shivers through his spine. His father had died of complications related to his bout of diabetes. The deterioration and subsequent shutdown of his body's key systems was noticeably grueling for him and painful to endure for his father as well as the entire family. Bob then pledged 1 percent of all his profits to the foundation; of his company's annual $1 billion profit that percentage would be his first $10 million. That was a seriously good start—a tenfold trouncing of the OneForOne Million Challenge! He talked to a few of his buddies and convinced them that SuperDuper Diabetes Research Institute, funded by his foundation, directed by him and assembling the top experts in the field, would be able to create the world's largest research institute with a single goal—to find a cure for diabetes in less than ten years. Bob's peers were amazed and interested; within months his buddies were taking similar initiatives to help drive funds to his foundation. They wrote cheques, gave speeches and openly supported Bob's efforts. Within a couple of years, Bob had established the largest private research institute dedicated solely to the efforts to cure diabetes.

This isn't far-fetched. I know that more than one of you out there is financially capable of this and has the desire and skills. You just have to put them into action.

This is a call to action for those of you who have read my book and others with whom you will share this book. I am challenging you to make a difference, to somehow figure out what you as one person can do to influence one million. You might start by setting a goal to raise one million dollars for a cause. Your effort might be to support the education of one million kids through some global or domestic program. How about giving a million pets, in shelters across North America, a new home? You could join forces with many local food banks and assemble a million meals for the hungry. What about sending a million malaria pills to Third World countries? How about conserving a million acres of ecologically sensitive land? Or how about devoting your life's work to eradicating disease(s) that affect millions of people annually? Oh yeah, and how about leveraging your influence to influence another million people to act? Any project will do.

But here's where accountability starts. As you knew before, or understand better now, philanthropy is not a token effort. A decision of this magnitude is life-changing. At first, it can be very unpopular with a lot of your peers or people around you. Your ideas might even ruffle feathers in the sector you decide that you would be best suited for and are passionate about. There might be people who have done things a certain way for a long time, and your ideas and innovation could put their livelihoods at risk. These all might be true, but you need to persevere.

Just think of when you began your most recent business venture. Was everyone pleased all the time? Or did you anger your competitors? Did your innovations disrupt tradition, or did your ideas raise eyebrows? This was not a deterrent for you; in fact, it was motivating. Sometimes the biggest "No" drove you to create your own "Yes," and others were compelled to follow your lead.

So How Do You Participate In the OneForOne Million Challenge?

Tell me about your OneForOne Million idea by visiting *www. InspiredProcess.com* or *www.OneForOneMillionChallenge.com*. Once your information has been registered, you will become part of a confidential philanthropic social enterprise study. The collective efforts of everyone who participates, no matter the size or scope, will change the world forever. I want to hear from you. I want to know what you have decided to do, how you have gone about it and why. I want to be there as a resource for you, to help you uncover answers to hard questions and to link you to the resources and people that might be able to help you succeed. You will not go it alone. We can share impassioned visions combined with objective viewpoints.

Our INSPIRED Process resources will uncover the best support for your efforts. We will help to link you with mentors or offer you opportunities to mentor others. We will provide you with needed social enterprise planning materials and business tools. Our network of educational groups can supply the governance and fiduciary training that will also support your organizational requirements.

With your permission we'll share your ideas (anonymously unless you are willing to be public), open the lines of communication and see if there are problems collective eyes might be able to solve. Sharing information, initiatives and innovations with others could provide a breakthrough, accelerate a discovery or begin a social movement. The depository of philanthropic ideas that you share will become a valuable resource.

As James Surowiecki, author of The Wisdom of Crowds, overwhelmingly highlighted in his book, the collective wisdom of many people adding their personal opinions, knowledge and experiences is most definitely more likely to arrive at the best solution—a smarter, more precise solution—for a given problem than that of the single smartest participant in that group. We will encourage the philanthropy of many people to uncover new ideas and better solutions to some of the biggest challenges of our time.

So join the OneForOne Million Challenge, send us your updates and ask for help. We'll track your progress and share whatever ideas you have that you think might help others who are pursuing their philanthropic dreams.

REFERENCES

1. *#234 Oprah Winfrey The World's Billionaires.* Forbes.com. Sept. 22, 2010. July 2010. http://www.forbes.com/lists/2009/10/ billionaires-2009-richest-people_Oprah-Winfrey_O0ZT.html

2. *About the Foundation – 15 Guiding Principles.* Bill & Melinda Gates Foundation. Sept. 22, 2010. July 2010. http://www.gates-foundation.org/about/Pages /overview.aspx

3. *Best of 2009: top 25 Tours.* Billboard. Dec. 13 2009. Sept. 22, 2010. http://www.billboard.com/news/top-25-tours-of-2009-1004053062.story

4. *Bill Clinton.* Wikimedia Foundation. Sept. 22, 2010. May 2010 – Aug. 2010. http://en.wikipedia.org/wiki/Bill_Clinton

5. *Bill Gates.* Wikimedia Foundation. Sept. 23 2010. May 2010 – Aug. 2010. http://en.wikipedia.org/wiki/Bill_Gates

    a. (Manes 1994, p. 11)

    b. Chapman, Glenn (June 27, 2008). "Bill Gates Signs Off". *Agence France-Presse.* http://afp.google.com/article/ALeqM5i8aV1bK5vmwLaw9wYr9nY5bFc4YA.

    c. Wahba, Phil (September 17, 2008). "Bill Gates tops U.S. wealth list 15 years in a row". Reuters. http://www.reuters.com/article/rbssTechMediaTelecomNews /idUSN 17 4 8882920080917. Retrieved November 6, 2008.

    d. "Flat-pack accounting". *The Economist.* May 11, 2006. http://www.economist.com/business/displaystory.cfm?story_id=6919139. Retrieved April 1, 2008.

    e. Cronin, Jon (January 25, 2005). "Bill Gates: billionaire philanthropist". *BBC News.* http://news.bbc.co.uk/2/hi/business/3913581.stm. Retrieved April 1, 2008.

    f.   "Our Approach to Giving". Bill & Melinda Gates Foundation. Archived from the original on April 4, 2008. http://web.archive.org/web/20080404212231/ http:// www.gates foundation .org/AboutUs/Our-Work/OurApproach/. Retrieved April 1, 2008

6. *Bob Geldof.* Wikimedia Foundation. Sept. 22 2010. May 2010 – Aug. 2010. http://en.wikipedia.org/wiki/Bob_Geldof

    a.   Analysis Section Staff Writer (29 July 2006). "Tell me why they don't like Geldof".

    b.   *Independant.*ie. http://www.independent.ie/opinion/ analysis/tell-me-why-they-dont-like-geldof-90194. html. Retrieved 2 July 2009.

    c.   Smith, David (30 January 2005). "We should share in 'Saint' Bob's Brit award, complain former Rats". *The Guardian* (London - The Observer home). http:// www.guardian.co.uk/uk/2005/jan/30/arts.artsnews1. Retrieved 30 June 2009.

    d.   Geldof, Bob (March 1987). *Is That It?* (First Edition ed.). London: Penguin. pp. 360 pages. ISBN 978-1555841157. http://www.amazon.co.uk/That-Bob-Geldof/dp /1555841155 /ref=ed_oe_h.

    e.   Staff Writer, BBC Radio 2 (21 December 2008). "Do They Know It's Christmas? Band Aid 20". (see also: http://www.bbc.co.uk/radio2/r2music/ documentaries/bandaid/) (BBC). Archived from the original on December 1, 2007. http://web.archive. org/web/20071201092115/http://www.gouk.com/ lordofmisrule/traditions/Band_Aid_1984_Do_They_ Know_Its_Christmas.htm. Retrieved 2 July 2009.

    f.   "Geldof nominated for Nobel Prize". BBC News. 6 July 2005. http://news.bbc.co.uk/2/hi/entertain-ment/4657627.stm. Retrieved 30 June 2009.

    g.   "Bob Geldof receives peace award". BBC News. 24 November 2005. http://news.bbc.co.uk/2/hi/enter-tainment/4466340.stm. Retrieved 30 June 2009.

h. "BBC on Ethiopian famine 1984". YouTube. http://
    www.youtube.com/watch?v=mj2jf0US8zI. Retrieved
    10 August 2010.

i. "Bono Among Nobel Peace Prize Nominees - San
    Francisco Chronicle". *San Francisco Chronicle*. http://
    www.sfgate.com/cgi-bin/article.cgi?file=/news/
    archive/2006 /02 /24/international/i082615S45.DTL.
    Retrieved 10 August 2010.

j. "Nominations for 2008 Nobels hits 197". *Brisbane
    Times*. 28 February 2008. http://news.brisbane-
    times.com.au/nominations-for-2008-nobels-
    hits-197/20080228-1vdy.html. Retrieved 10 August
    2010.

7. *Bono*. Wikimedia Foundation. Sept. 18, 2010. May 2010 – Aug.
   2010. http://en.wikipedia.org/wiki/Bono

    a. Macphisto.net. (2006). "U2 Biography—Bono". Re-
        trieved 3 May 2007, from MacPhisto.net

    b. Byrne, K. (Unknown last update). *U2 biography: Bono
        (from @U2)*. Retrieved 12 February 2007, from http://
        www.atu2.com/band/bono/index.html

    c. NBC Nightly News, "Brian Williams in Africa," May
        2007

    d. Lost Highway Records. (10 October 2005). "News".
        Retrieved 5 May 2007, retrieved on 12 December
        2008

    e. Denny, C., & Black, I. (15 March 2002). US and
        Europe boost aid to poorest countries. *The Guardian*.
        Retrieved 14 January 2007, from http://www.guard-
        ian.co.uk/international/story/0,3604,667739,00.html

    f. Unknown Author. (18 February 2003). Bono Among
        Nobel Peace Prize Nominees. *WNBC*. Retrieved 14
        January 2007, from Bono Among Nobel Peace Prize
        Nominees

g. Unknown Author. (25 February 2005). Bono given chance for Peace Prize. *The Scotsman*. Retrieved 14 January 2007, from http://news.scotsman.com/topics.cfm?tid=596&id=214402005 Scotsman.com

h. Langlois, F. (23 September 2004). John Ralston Saul awarded the Pablo Neruda International Presidential Medal of Honour. *Governor General of Canada*. Retrieved 14 January 2007, from http://www.gg.ca/media/doc.asp?lang=e&DocID=4267

i. "2004 TIME 100". *Time Magazine*. 26 April 2004. http://www.time.com/time/2004/time100/

j. "2006 TIME 100". *Time Magazine*: 84. 2006 http://www.time.com/time/2006/time100/

8. Clayton Hollingsworth, *Dragon's Den Higher Vibrations Wholistic Healing and Wellness*. CBC Television. Sept. 22, 2010. April 2010. http://www. cbc.ca/dragonsden /pitches/ higher-vibrations-wholistic-healing-and-wellness.html

9. Corporate Information: *Our Philosophy; Ten Things We Know To Be True #6*. Google. Sept. 9, 2010. July 2010. http://www.google.com/corporate/tenthings.html

10. Deepak Chopra, "Creating Affluence", Amber-Allen Publishing, 1998.

11. Don Martin, "Oilpatch brat pack hosts epic birthday bash Execs raise $3M for prostate cancer awareness. " *The National Post*. May 15, 2007.

BIBLIOGRAPHY

1. George McCully, "Philanthropy Reconsidered Private Initiatives: Public Good, Quality of Life." Boston: AuthorHouse, Aug. 27, 2008.

2. James Surowiecki, "The Wisdom of Crowds." First Anchor Books, 2005.

3. John and Miriam Carver, *Carver's Policy Governance** *Model in Non-profit Organizations*, John and Miriam Carver. Dec. 30, 2009. June 29, 2010. http://policygovernance.com/

4. Maddy Fry, *Bono Biography*. U2. Sept. 23, 2010. May 2010 – Aug. 2010 http://www.atu2.com/band/bono/

5. Marty Sulek, *On the Classical Meaning of Philanthropia, in Nonprofit and Voluntary Sector Quarterly* OnlineFirst, March 13, 2009 as doi:10.1177/0899764009333050

6. Melissa Brown. "Giving USA." Glenview: Giving USA Foundation, 2009.

7. Michael Hall *et al.*, "Caring Canadians, Involved Canadians: Highlights from the 2007 Canada Survey of Giving, Volunteering and Participating." Ottawa: Statistics Canada, June 8, 2009. http://www.givingandvolunteering.ca/files/giving/en/csgvp_highlights_2007.pdf.

8. *Oprah Winfrey*. Wikimedia Foundation. Sept. 23, 2010. May 2010 – Aug. 2010. http://en.wikipedia.org/wiki/Oprah_Winfrey

   a. Mowbray, Nicole (March 2, 2003). "Oprah's path to power". London: Guardian Unlimited. Retrieved August 25, 2008. http://www.guardian.co.uk/media/2003/mar/02/pressandpublishing.usnews1.

   b. Oprah.com, November 20, 2009.

    c.   Forbes.com. "Oprah Winfrey – The Forbes 400 Richest Americans". Forbes. http://www.forbes.com/profile/oprah-winfrey.

    d.   The 50 Most Generous Philanthropists.

9.   *Richard Branson.* Wikimedia Foundation. Sept. 22, 2010. May 2010 – Aug. 2010. http://en.wikipedia.org/wiki/Richard_Branson

    a.   Forbes.com. Retrieved 1 December 2008.

    b.   Forthcoming Marriages", *The Times*, 22 June 1949, pg.7.

    c.   "Famous people with Dyslexia". Dyslexiaonline.com. 30 March 2010. http://www.dyslexiaonline.com/famous/famous.htm. Retrieved 14 September 2010.

    d.   Global Elders (18 July 2007). "Nelson Mandela and Desmond Tutu Announce The Elders – An Historic Group of World Leaders". Press release. Retrieved 3 March 2009 http://dl.groovygecko.net/anon.groovy/clients/akqa/projectamber/press/The_Elders-Press_Release.pdf

10. *Richard Branson.* Virgin.com. Sept. 22, 2010. May 2010 – Aug. 2010. http://www.virgin.com/richard-branson/

11. Richard Branson, *Autobiography.* Virgin.com. Sept. 22, 2010. May 2010 – Aug. 2010. http://www.virgin.com/richard-branson/autobiography/

12. *The Giving Pledge.* Giving Pledge LLC. Sept. 24 2010. May 2010 – Aug. 2010. http://givingpledge.org/ and http://givingpledge.org/#enter.

13. *What We Do.* William J. Clinton Foundation. Sept. 24 2010. May 2010 – Aug. 2010. http://www.clintonfoundation.org/what-we-do/

14. William J. Clinton Foundation. Sept. 24 2010. May 2010 – Aug. 2010. http://www.clintonfoundation.org/

CPSIA information can be obtained at www.ICGtesting.com
Printed in the USA
LVOW06*1805051113

360112LV00016B/1402/P